Institute of Leadership
& Management

# **super**series

# Managing
# Health and
# Safety at Work

## FIFTH EDITION

Published for the
Institute of Leadership & Management

**ELSEVII**

...TON • HEIDELBERG • LONDON • NEW YORK • OXFORD
) • SAN FRANCISCO • SINGAPORE • SYDNEY • TOKYO
...non Flexible Learning is an imprint of Elsevier

**Pergamon**
*Flexible*
**Learning**

Pergamon Flexible Learning is an imprint of Elsevier
Linacre House, Jordan Hill, Oxford OX2 8DP, UK
30 Corporate Drive, Suite 400, Burlington, MA 01803, USA

First edition 1986
Second edition 1991
Third edition 1997
Fourth edition 2003
Fifth edition 2007

Editor:  David Pardey

Based on material in previous editions of this work

**British Library Cataloguing in Publication Data**
A catalogue record for this book is available from the British Library

**Library of Congress Cataloguing in Publication Data**
A catalogue record for this book is available from the Library of Congress

ISBN 978-0-08-046426-8

For information on all Pergamon Flexible Learning publications
visit our website at http://books.elsevier.com

Institute of Leadership & Management
Registered Office
1 Giltspur Street
London
EC1A 9DD
Telephone: 020 7294 2470
www.i-l-m.com
ILM is part of the City & Guilds Group

Typeset by Charon Tec Ltd (A Macmillan Company), Chennai, India
www.charontec.com
Printed and bound in Great Britain

07 08 09 10 11   10 9 8 7 6 5 4 3 2 1

# Contents

## Contents

# Session C   Accidents and their causes    61

# Session D   The management of safety    81

# Session E   Practical accident prevention    105

# Series preface

Whether you are a tutor/trainer or studying management development to further your career, Super Series provides an exciting and flexible resource to help you to achieve your goals. The fifth edition is completely new and up-to-date, and has been structured to perfectly match the Institute of Leadership & Management (ILM)'s new unit-based qualifications for first line managers. It also harmonizes with the 2004 national occupational standards in management and leadership, providing an invaluable resource for S/NVQs at Level 3 in Management.

Super Series is equally valuable for anyone tutoring or studying any management programmes at this level, whether leading to a qualification or not. Individual workbooks also support short programmes, which may be recognized by ILM as Endorsed or Development Awards, or provide the ideal way to undertake CPD activities.

For learners, coping with all the pressures of today's world, Super Series offers you the flexibility to study at your own pace to fit around your professional and other commitments. You don't need a PC or to attend classes at a specific time – choose when and where to study to suit yourself! And you will always have the complete workbook as a quick reference just when you need it.

For tutors/trainers, Super Series provides an invaluable guide to what needs to be covered, and in what depth. It also allows learners who miss occasional sessions to 'catch up' by dipping into the series.

Super Series provides unrivalled support for all those involved in first line management and supervision.

# Unit specification

| Title: | Managing health and safety at work | | Unit Ref: | M3.23 |
|---|---|---|---|---|
| **Level:** | 3 | | | |
| **Credit value:** | 2 | | | |

| Learning outcomes<br>*The learner* **will** | Assessment criteria<br>*The learner* **can** *(in an organization with which the learner is familiar)* | |
|---|---|---|
| 1. Understand health and safety at work | 1.1 | Identify *two* pieces of legislation relating to health, safety and welfare at work |
| | 1.2 | Explain *two* duties statute law imposes on both the manager and the team |
| | 1.3 | Outline the manager's responsibilities contained within the organization's Health and Safety Policy |
| | 1.4 | Explain the meaning of 'a competent person' |
| | 1.5 | Identify *two* ways to provide Health and Safety information, instruction and training to the team |
| | 1.6 | Identify expertise available in the organization to help and advise the manager on health and safety issues |
| 2. Understand risk assessment and accident prevention in the workplace | 2.1 | Conduct a simple risk assessment in the workplace |
| | 2.2 | Explain *one* practical accident prevention and control measure that could be implemented in the workplace |
| 3. Understand the organization's environmental responsibility | 3.1 | Explain the importance of environmental responsibility for your organization |
| | 3.2 | Describe what action the First Line Manager could take to enable the organization to fulfil its environmental responsibility |

# Workbook introduction

## 1 ILM Super Series study links

This workbook addresses the issues of *Managing Health and Safety at Work*. Should you wish to extend your study to other Super Series workbooks covering related or different subject areas, you will find a comprehensive list at the back of this book.

## 2 Links to ILM qualifications

This workbook relates to the learning outcomes of Unit M3.23 Managing health and safety at work from the ILM Level 3 Award, Certificate and Diploma in First Line Management.

## 3 Links to S/NVQs in management

This workbook relates to the following Unit of the Management Standards which are used in S/NVQs in Management, as well as a range of other S/NVQs:

E6. Ensure health and safety requirements are met in your area of responsibility

# 4 Workbook objectives

All managers need to know enough to ensure that the work activities they control remain within the requirements of the law. In the areas of health, safety and the environment, this is becoming increasingly difficult, because so many changes in the law have been made in recent times. Unfortunately, ignorance of the law is no defence, so it's of no avail to plead 'Nobody told me!'

As a first line manager, you should make it your job to learn as much about the law as you can, even if only to help you in planning your team's work.

Also, as a team leader, you have special responsibilities for the health and safety of your team members, as well as your own. Another good reason for studying the law on health and safety is that it provides guidance on minimum standards.

If you need one further reason for reading about the law, it is this. If you break the law, there is a real possibility that action could be taken against you, personally, as well as against your organization. This is especially likely to happen if a serious accident occurs as a result of your actions, or because of your failure to act. This workbook is divided into six sessions. Sessions A and B are devoted to health and safety aspects of the law, and Sessions C, D, E and F to risk assessment and accident prevention.

In Session A you will be able to read about the background to the law on health and safety. Session B goes on to describe the principal Acts and Regulations. Session C defines what we mean by 'accident', 'risk', 'hazard', and so on. After looking at a number of descriptions of accidents, we will try to identify some of the causes, and the means of preventing similar accidents. Session D examines safety from the point of view of management: costs; system strategies; legal obligations; risk assessment; people with a special role.

In Session E, we get down to practical accident prevention: analysing different types of accident, and identifying hazards common to many workplaces. Session F is entitled 'Coping with accidents'. It looks at the activities that must take place once an accident has occurred: emergency procedures, reporting, and investigation.

You don't want to expose your team members to danger. Accidents are costly (measured in both human and financial terms), disruptive, and morale destroying. If you've ever been involved in a serious accident yourself, or seen someone get hurt in one, you won't have forgotten it in a hurry.

As a manager, you have a responsibility to find ways of preventing accidents, and of minimizing the risks from hazards at your place of work. The philosophy of accident prevention is, in essence, simple: identify the hazards, and then put all necessary measures in place for eradicating them, or at the least, protecting people from them. As we will discuss, most accidents at work are the result of a failure to put this philosophy into practice in an adequate manner. In other words, accidents usually occur because the health and safety management system breaks down. To put it even more plainly: the majority of accidents could be prevented, if safety were better managed within the organization.

---

**Notes on studying this workbook.**

This book contains quite a lot of detail about health and safety and environmental legislation. You are not expected to remember it all. The best way to tackle the workbook is to read it through, completing the activities, and answering the self-assessment questions, in the usual way. You should be able to follow the points made, but don't feel you have to learn them all by heart.

Whenever you come across areas of law that seem particularly relevant to you and your job, make a note to remind yourself to find out more. There is a list of extensions at the back of the book, starting on page 172; alternatively, there may be people in your organization who can give you guidance.

---

# 4.1 Objectives

When you have completed this workbook you will be better able to:

- identify the most important laws related to health and safety;
- find out more about laws that are especially relevant to the work you do;
- explain to your team how the law affects them, and the duties imposed by the law on everyone at work;
- play your part in implementing and maintaining safe systems of work;
- identify hazards in your workplace, and take effective precautions against them;
- take part in risk assessment;
- identify some important points of health and safety law;
- cope with, report on and investigate accidents at work.

# 5 Activity planner

Activity 35 asks you to think about the status of your team's training on health and safety. It would be useful to identify beforehand what training the team has had.

For Activity 37, you are expected to give examples of identified hazards at your place of work, the results of the last risk assessment of these hazards, and to describe any further actions you plan to take with regard to them.

In Activity 50 you are asked to use a checklist to assess a particular manual handling operation. You should try to obtain a copy of the HSE booklet *Manual Handling – Guidance on Regulations*.

Activity 56 requires you to undertake a thorough review of the accident prevention measures currently in place in your work area, in respect of a chosen topic.

Some or all of these Activities may provide the basis of evidence for your S/NVQ portfolio. all Portfolio Activities and the Work-based assignment are signposted with this icon.

The icon states the elements to which the Portfolio Activities and Work-based assignment relate.

The Work-based assignment requires you to carry out a risk assessment. This task is designed to help you meet Unit E6. Ensure health and safety requirements are met in your area of responsibility.

# Session A
# Background to health and safety legislation

## 1 Introduction

Until well into the twentieth century, serious accidents and occupational hazards leading to disease were a normal part of working life for millions of the working population. People were made deaf by excessive noise in mills, burned by slag and molten metal in foundries, their lungs wrecked by dust in mining and farming, their organs poisoned by lead in paints or mercury used in making hats.

Many large rivers were so polluted that nothing could live in them. Air pollution, much of it from domestic chimneys, led to hundreds of deaths every year and illness for countless other people. 'Smogs' in London and most other towns and cities continued into the 1950s, bringing death and respiratory diseases to large numbers of people.

Standards have improved immensely since 1974. The point has now been reached where each successive improvement is harder to attain at affordable cost.

Laws to regulate working conditions began to be introduced in the nineteenth century. They tackled only the worst abuses, such as child labour and the employment of women and children in horrific conditions underground in mines.

Parliament finally did something about the state of the nineteenth century Thames when the stench became so unbearable that it was impossible to open windows. Thus the London sewerage system, which was still used well into the twentieth century, was built to assuage the discomfort of Members of Parliament.

Until the mid twentieth century, the health and safety of people at work continued to be poorly protected. Legislation was piecemeal, often following specific abuses or disasters.

## 1.1 The Health & Safety At Work, etc. Act 1974

The major turning point came in 1974, with the first comprehensive Health & Safety at Work, etc. Act (HSWA), which imposed a general duty of care on virtually every employer.

The Act imposes clear duties on employers relating to health, safety and welfare at work, and also provides guidance on how to promote high standards in these areas. It also imposes obligations on employees to take care for themselves and others who may be affected by their actions.

The opening sentence of the Act includes the word 'welfare':

> 'An Act to make further provision for securing the health, safety and *welfare* of persons at work . . .'

and it is important to keep this third aspect of the Act in mind when you are looking at health and safety issues at your workplace.

But we begin with a preface to our subject.

## 2 Introduction to health and safety legislation

We need to start by seeing health and safety in the context of the law in general.

## 2.1 Sources of law

The law applicable in the UK is derived from three principal sources:

Although Scottish law has continued to develop along different lines from English law since the Act of Union in 1703, and is partly derived from Scottish common law, all the Acts and regulations we will discuss in this workbook are also applicable in Scotland.

■ **statute law**

Acts of parliament, such as the Health and Safety at Work, etc. Act 1974, together with subordinate legislation (sometimes called 'statutory instruments'), such as the Management of Health and Safety at Work Regulations 1999.

■ **common law**

based on case law – the decisions made in courts over the centuries. Once a judgment is made, a **precedent** is established. A court is bound to follow earlier decisions made in higher courts, or in courts at the same level.

■ **contract law**

governing agreements between two parties. Contract law does not play much part in health and safety.

Most health and safety law has been created through statute law.

Under common law, an action might be brought for the tort of 'negligence', which may be defined as:

> 'the omission to do something which a reasonable person would do, or doing something which a prudent or reasonable person would not do'.

To prove negligence, the injured party, or plaintiff, must prove that:

■ a duty of care existed on the part of the defendant towards the plaintiff;
■ the defendant has breached that duty by behaving in a way in which a reasonable person would not behave;
■ the plaintiff must have suffered some damage.

## 2.2 Civil law and criminal law

Both criminal law and civil law are important to organizations in terms of health and safety.

Anyone committing a crime has offended against the State, and is in breach of criminal law. If an organization fails to comply with its statutory health and safety duties, then it or its officers may be prosecuted under criminal law. If guilt is proved 'beyond reasonable doubt', the offender may be punished by the court by having a fine imposed. In theory at least, jail sentences can also be passed on individuals.

Under civil actions, a plaintiff sues a defendant, usually for damages, that is, financial compensation. As an example, an individual may sue an employer if he or she is injured at work. A lesser standard of proof applies in civil actions than in criminal prosecutions: cases have to be proved 'on the balance of probabilities', rather than 'beyond reasonable doubt'.

Activity 1 · 2 mins

Briefly describe the **two** main ways in which organizations may have legal actions brought as a result of an accident at work.

_____

_____

_____

_____

The following diagram shows the possible routes that could be taken through the legal system, following an accident at work.

The two main routes are through the civil and criminal courts. The third route, shown on the right of the diagram, is via an employment tribunal.

EXTENSION 1
This table is taken from
_Health and Safety Law_ by
Jeremy Stranks.

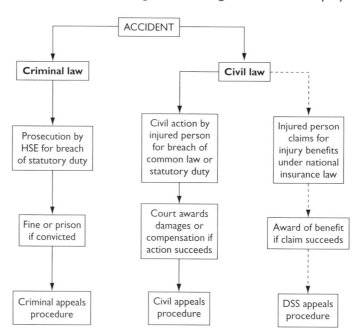

Redrawn, with kind permission, from a diagram in _Health and Safety Law_, by Jeremy Stranks

## 2.3 European law

The United Kingdom is a member State of the European Union (EU), along with 14 other nations: Austria, Belgium, Denmark, Finland, France, Germany, Greece, Holland, Ireland, Italy, Luxembourg, Portugal, Spain and Sweden.

Although we still make our own laws in the UK, membership of the EU has had a profound effect on our laws and lawmaking. One important fact is that, if ever there is any conflict, European laws take precedence over national laws in the courts.

The two principal instruments by which the European Union makes laws are:

- **EU Regulations** that apply directly in all member countries. Actions based on EU Regulations can be brought in national courts. (EU Regulations should not be confused with UK Regulations, many of which we will discuss in this workbook.)
- **Directives**, which bind member countries to comply with an agreed ruling. Unlike EU Regulations, Directives are normally made into national laws by each State. A good deal of modern health and safety legislation is the direct result of EU Directives.

The **Single European Act** was made law at the beginning of 1993. Its aim is to eliminate technical barriers to trade by introducing a new approach to technical harmonization and standards. Largely as a result of this Act, national standards for health and safety within the Union are being made to conform with one another.

Much of the environmental law either proposed or already in force stems from the European Union.

## 2.4 Approved codes of practice and guidance notes

These two kinds of document are useful sources of information about the law.

**Approved Codes of Practice (ACOPs)** are issued by the Health and Safety Commission (HSC) as interpretations of Regulations, and are intended to help people apply the law in practice. ACOPs are designed to:

- make Regulations more plain or more specific;
- explain how Regulations can be complied with in a satisfactory way.

## Example

Regulation 15 of the Workplace (Health, Safety and Welfare) Regulations 1992 states that:

1 No window, skylight or ventilator which is capable of being opened shall be likely to be opened, closed or adjusted in a manner which exposes any person performing such operation to a risk to his health or safety.

2 No window, skylight or ventilator shall be in a position when open which is likely to expose any person in the workplace to a risk to his health or safety.

Part of the ACOP for this regulation says:

153 It should be possible to reach and operate the control of openable windows, skylights and ventilators in a safe manner. Where necessary, window poles or similar equipment should be kept available, or a stable platform or other safe means of access should be provided. Controls should be so placed that people are not likely to fall through or out of the window. Where there is a danger of falling from a height, devices should be provided to prevent the window opening too far.

---

**Guidance notes** may also be issued, either by the Health and Safety Commission (HSC) or the Health and Safety Executive (HSE). They include, for example, advice on action to be taken by employers in order to conform with the law.

To summarize this introduction:

■ the three sources of law are statute law, common law and contract law;
■ it's important to distinguish between criminal law and civil law, and there is a separate court system for each; however, both are important in health and safety;
■ the UK's membership of the European Union has had a profound effect on our environmental, health and safety legislation;
■ useful documents that are intended to help people apply the law are Approved Codes of Practice (ACOPs) and guidance notes.

# 3 The Health and Safety at Work, etc. Act, 1974 (HSWA)

EXTENSION 2
*Workplace health, safety and welfare: a short guide for managers* is available from HSE Books.

The Health and Safety at Work, etc. Act 1974 (HSWA) is the most important safety legislation ever to come into force in the UK. It is an 'enabling' Act which 'enables' Ministers (that is gives them the power) to introduce Regulations, called 'Statutory Instruments' and 'Approved Codes of Practice' (ACOPs) which explain in far more detail how the general provisions of the Act are to be implemented. While the enabling Act itself does not need to be changed or updated except in extremely unusual circumstances, Ministers can update Regulations and ACOPs that have been created under the Act whenever they think it necessary. These Regulations and ACOPs are discussed in detail in Session B.

Under HSWA, three separate bodies exist to promote health, safety and welfare on a continuing basis. These bodies are the HSC, HSE and EMAS.

## 3.1 Health and Safety Commission (HSC)

The Health and Safety Commission (HSC) is a body that includes representatives from all interested parties, including industry and the trades unions, under a 'chair' appointed by the Secretary of State. The Commission advises the Government on long-term issues and makes strategic recommendations for the continuous improvement of standards.

The HSC publishes comprehensive data every year, available from HSE Books.

## 3.2 Health and Safety Executive (HSE)

The Health and Safety Executive (HSE) is charged with enforcing the law through its inspectors, who have wide powers to investigate incidents and accidents and who can serve prohibition orders and enforcement notices on defaulting organizations. Local authorities also have responsibility for some aspects of enforcement.

### The HSE's role in accident reporting and investigation – the 'RIDDOR' Regulations

If an organization's health and safety standards are to be continuously imposed, it is essential for them to have accurate, up-to-date information on incidents and accidents that have occurred. The UK's data are as good as any in the world and are obtained under the Reporting of Injuries, Diseases and Dangerous Occurrences Regulations of 1995 (RIDDOR).

The Regulations demand that a 'responsible person', normally the person in control of the afflicted site, reports what has happened on a prescribed form to the HSE or, sometimes, to the Local Authority.

Safety representatives have a statutory right to review these reports and to investigate the circumstances. In Session B you will find details of the categories that must be reported and that form the basis for statistics published by the HSC. Safety Committees will consider such reports as a standing item on their agendas.

## 3.3 Employment Medical Advisory Service (EMAS)

The Employment Medical Advisory Service (EMAS) provides information and advice to the Government, employers and employees on medical matters affecting employment.

Activity 2 · 2 mins

Who in law do you think would have duties under HSWA?

_____

_____

_____

Both employers and employees have duties under HSWA.

Let's look at the duties of the employer first.

## 3.4 The employer's overall duties under HSWA

Under HSWA, an employer has a duty:

'to ensure, as far as reasonably practicable, the health, safety and welfare at work of all his employees'.

The key words in the extract are **'as far as reasonably practicable'**. This is the 'yardstick' by which an employer's actions will be judged.

We will discuss what 'as far as reasonably practicable' means in the next section.

To do this, the employer will need to be sure that (to give a few examples):

- plant and equipment are safely installed, operated and maintained;
- systems of work are checked frequently, to ensure that risks from hazards are minimized;
- the work environment is regularly monitored to ensure that people are protected from any toxic contaminants;
- safety equipment is inspected regularly;
- risks to health from natural and artificial substances are minimized.

HSWA also places an obligation on employers to take care of the health and safety of non-employees.

# Activity 3

3 mins

Can you suggest **two** groups of people, other than employees, that an employer may have duties towards under health and safety laws?

_____

_____

_____

_____

_____

_____

You may have mentioned:

- self-employed people or contractors' employees working on site;
- customers who visit (for instance) shop or garage premises;
- visiting suppliers;
- other visitors;
- the general public living and working outside the worksite.

# 3.5 Health & Safety Policy Statement

The HSWA requires all employers with five or more employees to prepare, publish and keep up to date a statement of the organization's general policy towards health and safety at work.

The clear intention is that the Policy as set out is a practical document that will ensure that there is a 'progressive improvement in health and safety performance' (Management of Health and Safety at Work Regulations, approved Code of Practice). The requirements are as follows.

## General Policy Statement

This must:

- **state clearly** what the organization's policy is, for example 'to protect the health, safety and welfare of all employees, contractors, visitors and customers while they are at work or on its premises'. Account may also need to be taken of neighbouring sites that may be affected by the organization's activities;
- **require acceptance** of the Policy by all personnel, including acceptance of the need for safety training;
- **commit** the organization to improving safety performance continuously.

## Organization and arrangements

These need to:

- **identify specifically** the responsibilities of office holders, such as the chief executive and other executives, and specialist advisors, such as safety officers and occupational health professionals;
- **specify resources** that will be provided to implement the policy, including those required for systematic training of personnel;
- **state** who is responsible for publishing the policy and keeping it up to date.

# Activity 4

**S/NVQ E6**

Obtain a copy of your own organization's Health and Safety Policy. Compare it with the general requirements indicated here and then use it to answer the following questions.

In your organization, who is responsible for issuing the Policy?

_____

Who is responsible for providing resources to implement it?

_____

What responsibilities are assigned to all general employees?

_____

What mention is made of visitors, contractors' employees, customers and neighbouring sites?

_____

If you have any problem obtaining the Policy Statement or obtaining the information, please talk to your manager.

## 3.6 The employee's duties under HSWA

Under HSWA, employees have a duty:

- to take reasonable care to avoid injury to themselves or to others by their work activities;
- to co-operate with employers and others in meeting the requirements of the law including the acceptance of health and safety training; and
- not to interfere with or misuse anything provided to protect their health, safety and welfare.

# Activity 5

Kenny works for a contractor who is replacing paving slabs and kerbstones in a busy market place. He has to cut the slabs using power tools, which create dust and noise. The work must be carried out while the market is working and in all weathers. His work mates and many members of the public are likely to be in the general area as well.

Kenny's employer has a duty to do everything 'which is reasonably practicable' to ensure his safety. But what steps should Kenny take to ensure the safety of:

■  himself;
■  his working colleagues;
■  the general public.

Kenny

_____

_____

His working colleagues

_____

_____

The general public

_____

_____

The list of items you have noted will probably include the following:

To ensure his safety, Kenny should:

■  wear all protective clothing as he is trained and instructed to do, including ear defenders, eye protection and safety footwear;
■  check equipment and use it only if it is in safe working condition and he is trained and authorized to use it;
■  use equipment only for the purpose intended, and using all the guards, noise and dust control devices specified;
■  take account of weather and site conditions.

To ensure the safety of his working colleagues, Kenny should:

- check that they will not be adversely affected by noise, dust or fumes;
- store materials and offcuts safely, to ensure that he does not create tripping hazards;
- position any designated safety barriers as required and work within them.

To ensure the safety of the general public, Kenny should:

- take the same safety measures as for his colleagues;
- remember that certain people, such as children and the elderly, may not be aware of hazards, and that they do not have ear defenders, etc. provided to them;
- ensure that his work is confined by safety barriers and that the public is protected from dust, flying particles and excessive noise.

# Activity 6

4 mins

Jot down **three** things you would expect a member of **your** team to do, or **not** do, in order to help ensure the safety of others.

_____

_____

_____

_____

_____

Your response will be relevant to the kind of job you do. In general, you might expect a team member:

- to think of the safety and health of others when carrying out his or her job

For example, Kenny would be expected to protect his workmates and members of the general public from the noise, dust and fumes he will create. In another kind of job, a typist in an office would be expected to make sure that cables, boxes and other obstacles are not a hazard to people walking by.

- to behave sensibly and responsibly in matters of health and safety

  For instance, it would be irresponsible for someone to cover up a safety notice, or to use a fire bucket for another purpose, or to prop open a fire door that should be kept closed.

- not to indulge in 'horseplay' or practical jokes

  The team leader sometimes has to take care that a 'harmless bit of fun' is not allowed to turn into something more dangerous. A good leader will make plain what is allowed and what isn't.

- to obey the rules of the organization

  People tend to break safety rules for many reasons. For example, because:

  - they aren't aware of the rules;
  - they don't see any point in the rules;
  - the rules impose conflicting restrictions, such as slowing down a process which the person wants to complete as quickly as possible: there is often a great temptation to 'cut corners';
  - they see other people, such as managers and external contractors, ignoring the rules, and follow their bad example.

## Activity 7 · 3 mins

Can you think of an instance where someone in your team has been tempted to cut corners in a job, and thereby has compromised safety? If so, describe it briefly.

_____

_____

_____

_____

_____

_____

_____

Depending on the kind of work you are in, you may have suggested some of the following.

■ Not bothering to put on protective clothing.

> 'I know I should have worn a safety helmet, but I was only going to be out in the yard for two minutes. How was I to know that it would be slippery and that I would fall and crack my head open?' (Man speaking from hospital bed.)

■ Not using the right equipment.

> 'The step ladder was in use at the time, and I only wanted one item from the top shelf to finish the whole job. Now it looks like I'll be off work for three months.' (Woman on crutches.)

■ Not isolating equipment before working on it.

> 'Yes, I admit that I should have checked that the electrical power was off before I asked young Peter to open the fuse-box. I was thinking about how much time the interruption was costing us. Now I'll have to live with this for the rest of my life.' (Supervisor at inquiry into fatal accident.)

■ Working on, knowing the risks, and choosing to ignore them for one reason or another.

> 'The only way to get to the lift control box is to stick your head into the shaft. I suppose we should have shut down the system – but we'd been told that two people were trapped in the lift between floors. We've never had an accident till now. It was a succession of events that caused it. First of all the lift wasn't faulty at all – it was just that one of the doors wasn't shut properly. The trapped people got out, but no one told us. Then someone must have knocked down the warning notice on the ground floor, and somebody else used the lift just at the time Jim was leaning into the shaft. He didn't stand a chance when that balancing weight came down.' (Maintenance engineer talking after fatal accident.)

To sum up:

- Employees have responsibilities under HSWA:

  - to take care for their own health and safety, and that of their colleagues;
  - to co-operate in meeting the requirements of the law;
  - not to interfere with or misuse anything provided to protect their health, safety and welfare.

- People who cut corners endanger themselves and others.

# 4 Levels of statutory duty

In law, there are three separate levels of statutory duty. From the lowest to the highest, they are:

- 'reasonably practicable' requirements;
- 'practicable' requirements;
- 'absolute' requirements.

Let's discuss what each of these means.

## 4.1 The duty to act in a 'reasonably practicable' manner

You will recall that a key phrase, repeated many times in the Health and Safety at Work, etc. Act 1974, is 'as far as reasonably practicable'.

To illustrate what is 'reasonably practicable' so far as health and safety is concerned, read the following case.

Some new partitions were being erected in an open-plan office by contractors. The work was dusty and noisy, even though it had been screened off. The main route from the office to the cloakrooms and rest room was affected. The remaining passageway was narrow, dark and crossed by trailing leads. Some building materials were being stored 'temporarily' in it.

Several staff complained to their team leader, demanding that she 'do something about it before someone gets hurt'. She replied that 'It's only for a few days' and they 'should just be extra careful'.

# Activity 8 ·

4 mins

In your opinion:

- are the staff's requests for action justified?
- was their team leader acting in a 'reasonably practicable' way by telling them to ignore the problem because it was 'only for a few days'?

_____

_____

_____

It is reasonable for the staff to complain. Tripping is a major cause of accidents. In a 'few days' it would be quite possible for someone to trip over leads or materials stored in a narrow, dark passage on a busy route. It would be 'reasonably practical' for the team leader, either directly or with help from her manager, to demand that the materials be moved out of the passage, that trailing leads be re-routed safely and that temporary lighting be rigged safely. The cost would be minimal and proportionate to the benefits gained.

This case was perhaps not too difficult to make a judgement about. Other situations may not be so straightforward. The expression 'so far as is reasonably practicable' has only acquired a clear meaning through many interpretations by the courts.

According to the Health and Safety Executive:

EXTENSION 3
This extract and the one below, is from _Successful Health and Safety Management,_ published by HSE Books.

- 'To carry out a duty so far as is reasonably practicable means that **the degree of risk** in a particular activity or environment **can be balanced against the time, trouble, cost and physical difficulty of taking measures to avoid the risk**.

- If these are so disproportionate to the risk that it would be unreasonable for the persons concerned to have to incur them to prevent it, they are not obliged to do so.

- **The greater the risk the more likely it is that it is reasonable to go to very substantial expense, trouble and invention to reduce it**. But if the consequences and the extent of a risk are small, insistence on great expense would not be considered reasonable.

- It is important to remember that the judgement is an objective one and **the size or financial position of the employer are immaterial.**'

## 4.2 'Practicable' requirements

The phrase 'so far as is practicable' – without the qualifying word 'reasonably' – implies a stricter standard. The interpretation of the phrase given by HSE is as follows.

> 'This term generally embraces **whatever is technically possible** in the light of current knowledge, which the person concerned had, or ought to have had, at the time. The **cost, time, and trouble involved are not to be taken into account.**'

## 4.3 'Absolute' requirements

In health and safety Regulations, such as those we will discuss in the next section, the words 'shall' or 'must' are used frequently. In these cases, there can be no argument or interpretation: the law **must** be obeyed.

### Example

Regulation 7 (page 26) of the Health and Safety (Display Screen Equipment) Regulations 1992 states that:

1 Every employer **shall** ensure that operators and users at work in his undertaking are provided with adequate information about –

   a  all aspects of health and safety relating to their workstations; and

   b  such measures taken by him in compliance with his duties under regulations 2 and 3 as relate to them and their work.

In brief, for all employers:

- 'reasonably practicable' means that the degree of risk has to be balanced against the cost, time and difficulty of taking measures to avoid the risk;
- 'practicable' means that the cost, time and difficulty are not to be considered – technical feasibility is the only consideration;
- 'absolute' – often indicated by the word 'shall' – means that the law **must** be obeyed.

Before going on to look at how the health and safety law is enforced, you need to be aware of another important Act that is in force in parallel with HSWA. This is the Fire Precautions Act 1971.

# 5 Fire Precautions Act 1971

This Act governs fire safety at most non-domestic premises in the UK.

The Act's basic requirement is that all premises that meet certain criteria must hold a current Fire Certificate, kept and displayed prominently on the site. Such premises include:

■ most hotels and boarding houses;
■ offices, shops, factories and railway premises where:

  ■ more than 20 people work at any one time; or
  ■ more than ten people are employed at any one time other than on the ground floor; or
  ■ the premises are part of a larger building which meets either of the first two conditions; or
  ■ explosives or highly flammable materials are stored or used.

A valid Fire Certificate will specify:

■ the use or uses of the site, the means of escape from it (usually indicated on a plan) and how this will be kept usable at all times;
■ how a fire may be fought – including sprinkler systems and localized equipment;
■ warning systems, emergency and evacuation procedures and training to be given to staff.

# 6 Enforcing the law

It is the job of the Health and Safety Inspectorate or, in some smaller businesses, Environmental Health Officers, to enforce the law.

Inspectors have wide-reaching powers. These include the right to:

■ enter and inspect any premises, at any time, where it is considered that there may be dangers to health or safety;
■ be accompanied by any duly authorized person, such as a policeman or a doctor;
■ enquire into the circumstances of accidents;

■ require that facilities and assistance be provided by anyone able to give them;
■ take statements;
■ require that areas be left undisturbed;
■ collect evidence, take photographs, make measurements, and so on;
■ take possession of articles;
■ require the production of books and documents.

To enforce certain actions, an inspector can:

■ issue a **prohibition notice**, which stops – with immediate effect – people from carrying on activities which are considered to involve a risk of serious personal injury;
■ issue an **improvement notice**, which compels an employer to put right conditions that contravene the law, within a specified time period;
■ initiate **prosecutions**, especially in the case of repeated, deliberate or severe offences.

It goes without saying that managers are expected to give their full co-operation to the enforcing authorities.  The liability for personal prosecutions is very real.

An employer can appeal against an improvement notice or a prohibition notice. Here is an example of the case one company put up against a prohibition notice. The prohibition notice was issued to prevent a cutting machine being used, because a safety guard had been removed.

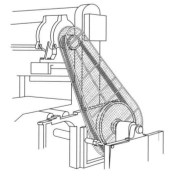

From HSE book *Work Equipment – Guidance on Regulations*

The guard was removed to enable the machine to cope with an oversize order which was successfully completed. When the guard was removed the electronic cut-out mechanism, which would normally stop the machine running without the guard, was damaged.

The manufacturers of the electronic components for this type of guard have gone out of business, and it will take some time to find a suitable alternative, although the company is making every effort to do so.

To have a cut-out mechanism made specially would be very expensive.

The company is appealing against the prohibition notice on the grounds of cost and difficulty.

# Activity 9

Imagine you have to make a judgement on this appeal. You understand that cost and difficulty is an important consideration for any organization, but your main concern is that of safety.

Would you agree that the prohibition should be lifted, given the circumstances?                                                                    YES/NO

Give a brief reason for your answer.

_____

_____

_____

_____

_____

_____

In spite of the cost and difficulties, there is not sufficient reason to lift the prohibition notice. Safety must come first. If the company were to use the machine without a guard, or with a guard that could be removed easily because there is no cut-out mechanism, someone might be seriously injured.

It is in fact very difficult to make a successful appeal against a prohibition notice or an improvement notice.

# 7 Safety representatives and committees

Everyone has a part to play in health and safety matters. It seems sensible for an employer, therefore, to encourage employee participation in this area.

EXTENSION 4
If you are interested in this subject, you may want to read the Health and Safety Commission booklet *Safety Representatives and Safety Committees*.

In this section, we'll take a brief look at the role of safety representatives and safety committees in health and safety.

The regulations covering safety representatives and safety committees are included in Section 15 of HSWA and in the Safety Representatives and Safety Committees Regulations 1977.

## 7.1 The safety representative

A safety representative is someone appointed by a recognized trade union to represent employees on health and safety matters at work. Because they need to be familiar with the hazards of the workplace and the work being done, safety representatives are usually people with two or more years' experience in that particular job.

Safety representatives have three main functions. The first one is to take all reasonably practicable steps to keep themselves informed.

## Activity 10 · 4 mins

What kind of information do you think an employees' representative on health and safety would need, in order to do a good job?

_____

_____

_____

_____

Safety representatives would surely need to be familiar with:

■ what the law says about the health and safety of people at work, and particularly the people they represent;
■ the particular hazards of the workplace;
■ the measures needed to eliminate these hazards, or to cut down the risk from them;
■ the employer's health and safety policy, and the organization and arrangements for putting that policy into practice.

The second main function is to encourage co-operation between their employer and employees so that:

- measures can be developed and promoted to ensure the health and safety of employees;
- the effectiveness of these measures can be checked.

The third function is to bring to the attention of the employer any unsafe or unhealthy conditions or working practices, or unsatisfactory welfare arrangements.

## Activity 11

Knowing the functions of a safety representative, you may be able to work out the kind of activities involved. Jot down **two** possible activities, if you can.

_____

_____

_____

_____

As you may have mentioned, safety representatives will usually be involved in:

- talking to employees about particular health and safety problems;
- carrying out inspections of the workplace to see whether there are any real or potential hazards that haven't been adequately addressed;
- reporting to employers about these problems and other matters connected to health and safety in that workplace;
- taking part in accident investigations.

Inspections and reports should be recorded formally in writing.

# 7.2 Safety committees

An employer is legally obliged to set up a safety committee after receiving written requests to do so from two safety representatives.

It is good practice for **all** employers to operate a safety committee, and nowadays a very large number do, whether or not they have been requested to do so by safety representatives.

Ideally, a site safety committee should comprise:

- a senior manager for the site who is **not** a safety specialist and who chairs the committee;
- representatives from all key departments;
- union safety representatives (where they have been appointed);
- specialist employees, including engineers, medical staff, risk managers, safety professionals – according to the organization's structure;
- external specialists and advisors on an 'occasional' basis.

Larger sites may have a number of departmental committees as well as a site committee.

The safety committee:

- reviews the organization's health and safety rules and procedures;
- studies statistics and trends of accidents and health problems;
- considers reports and information received from health and safety inspectors;
- keeps a watch on the effectiveness of the safety content of employee training.

Let's look at the kind of accident statistics that might typically be collected in an organization.

# Activity 12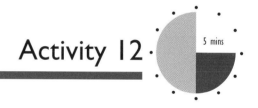

5 mins

Read through the accident statistics on page 25 and try to spot **three** facts that might be of interest to a safety committee.

_____

_____

_____

_____

_____

_____

## Portdown Engineering (Bosham) Ltd.
## ACCIDENT STATISTICS SHEET

**Period:** From 23.03     To 19.04

| Date of accident | Length of service | Name, clock no. and department | Sex | Age | Occupation | Description of accident | Nature of injury | Absent (days) | Code |
|---|---|---|---|---|---|---|---|---|---|
| 25.03 | 7 yrs 6 mths | J.P. Peters Blownware Factory | F | 41 | Inspector | While inspecting glass in the Blownware factory a flask exploded causing injury. | Cut right forearm. | 6 | 1/14 |
| 09.04 | 3 mths | C.K. Rush Packing Dept. | F | 22 | Packer | While packing glass and using stapler machine she felt pain in her neck. | Pain in neck. | 5 | 14 |
| 19.04 | 4 yrs 10 mths | J.C. Isoz Packing Dept. | M | 32 | Packer | While packing glass he developed pains in both arm and back. | Pain in arms and back. | 10 | 14 |
| 26.03 | 4 yrs 4 mths | S.J. Ruffle Deptford Dec' Cent. | F | 43 | Packer | While lifting glass from crate she strained her back. | Back strain. | 15 | 5 |
| 23.03 | 1 mth | I.T. Hones Packing Dept. | M | 17 | Packer | While packing glass, a roll of shrink wrap material, standing on end, fell over and hit foot. | Bruised right big toe. | 13 | 5 |
| 10.04 | 6 yrs 5 mths | A.L. Carvell Deepdale Dept. | F | 37 | Inspector | While opening cartons to inspect contents, she cut bend of small finger causing injury. | Very small cut to small finger of left hand. | 2 | 1/14 |
| 03.04 | 2 yrs 8 mths | J.Y. Blincowe Plant and Services | M | 62 | Steel erector | While walking outside of Steel erector shop, he twisted his ankle. | Injury to right outer ankle. | 9 | 14 |
| 23.03 | 1 yr | D.M. Hussein Receiving Stores | M | 25 | Labourer | While loading laundry onto trailer, he caught his knee on edge of trailer. | Pain in right knee. | 16 | 4 |
| 07.04 | 8 yrs 3 mths | J. Austin Transport | M | 48 | Driver | While trailer was being parked at Deptford parking area, he was jammed between unit and wall. | Fractures to right collar bone, right arm and foot. | 27 | 5 |
| 13.04 | 6 mths | G.I.K. Shemwell Transport | M | 39 | Fork lift driver | While loading pallets into trailer in Pressware Factory, he felt pain in his back. | Pain in lumbar region of back. | 10 | 5 |

A safety committee may have noted that in less than a month:

- there was one **major injury** (involving both a fractured collar bone and a fractured arm) as defined under the RIDDOR Regulations (see Session B) and a potentially very serious accident (exploding flask);
- there were nine accidents involving absence from work of more than three days;
- several accidents involved lifting and handling operations;
- several relatively minor injuries resulted in several days off work;
- three new members of staff were involved in accidents;
- there was no 'near miss' data or data about accidents causing damage to property, equipment or stock; or accidents not causing lost time. This suggested that such incidents were not being reported.

> Note that HSE must be notified whenever a person at work is incapacitated for normal work for more than three days as a result of an injury caused by an accident at work.

This short section should have given you an idea of the functions of safety representatives and safety committees.

You may also want to note the following point of law. Under the Trade Union Reform and Employment Rights Act 1993 and the Public Interest Disclosure Act 1999, all employees, regardless of their length of service, have a right to complain to an employment tribunal if they are dismissed or victimized for:

- carrying out any health and safety activities for which they have been designated by their employer;
- performing any functions as an official or employer-acknowledged health and safety representative or safety committee member;
- bringing a reasonable health and safety concern to their employer's attention in the absence of a representative or committee who could do so on their behalf;
- leaving their work area or taking other appropriate action in the face of serious and imminent danger.

# Self-assessment 1

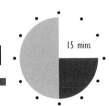

15 mins

1  Pick the correct statements from among the following.

a  Statute law is derived from court decisions.  ❏

b  Contract law is relatively unimportant in health and safety matters.  ❏

c  Following an accident, an organization may be prosecuted under either criminal law or civil law.  ❏

d  European law takes precedence over UK law.  ❏

e  The Health and Safety at Work, etc. Act 1974 is a disabling Act.  ❏

f  The Health and Safety at Work, etc. Act 1974 places an obligation on employers to take care of the health and safety of customers on its premises.  ❏

g  Employees have duties to co-operate with employers in meeting the requirements of the law.  ❏

h  If an employee is given defective equipment, and gets hurt as a result, it's entirely the employer's fault.  ❏

i  'As far as reasonably practicable' means that the degree of risk can be balanced against the cost of taking measures to avoid the risk.  ❏

j  'So far as is practicable' means that the degree of risk can be balanced against the cost of taking measures to avoid the risk.  ❏

2  The following statements about safety representatives have some words missing. Fill in the blanks from the words listed below.

Safety representatives may be involved in:

ACCIDENT        CO-OPERATION
HAZARDS         INSPECTIONS
PRACTICES       REPORTING
TALKING         UNSAFE
WELFARE         WORKPLACE

- _____ to employees about particular health and safety problems;

- encouraging _____ between their employer and employees;

- carrying out _____ of the workplace to see whether there are any real or potential _____ that haven't been adequately addressed;

- bringing to the attention of the employer any _____ or unhealthy conditions or working _____, or unsatisfactory _____ arrangements;

- _____ to employers about these problems and other matters connected to health and safety in that _____;

- taking part in _____ investigations.

3  Match the correct description from the list on the right with each term on the left.

| | |
|---|---|
| a Approved codes of practice (ACOPs) | i Acts of Parliament (such as the Health and Safety at Work, etc. Act 1974), together with a great many 'statutory instruments' or 'subordinate legislation'. |
| b Civil law | ii Stops, with immediate effect, people from carrying out activities that are considered to involve a risk of serious personal injury. |
| c Prohibition notice | iii Anyone committing a crime has offended against the state, and is in breach of this. If an organization fails to comply with its statutory health and safety duties, its officers may be prosecuted. |
| d Criminal law | iv A plaintiff sues a defendant, usually for damages, that is, financial compensation. As an example, an individual may sue an employer if he or she is injured at work. |
| e EU Directives | v Compels an employer to put right conditions that contravene the health and safety law. |
| f Improvement notice | vi Bind member countries to comply with an agreed ruling. They are normally made into national laws by each state. |
| i Statute law | vii Issued by the Health and Safety Commission (HSC) as interpretations of regulations, and are intended to help people apply the law in practice. |

Answers to these questions can be found on page 176.

# 8 Summary

- The law applicable in the UK is derived from three principal sources: statute law, common law, and contract law.

- Although it is important to distinguish between civil law and criminal law, both are important to organizations in terms of health and safety.

- Following an accident, actions may be brought against an organization through the criminal courts (for breach of statutory duty); through the civil courts (for breach of common law or statutory duty); or through an employment tribunal (for injury benefits).

- European laws take precedence over national laws in the courts, if ever there is any conflict.

- Approved Codes of Practice (ACOPs) are issued by the Health and Safety Commission (HSC) as interpretations of Regulations, and are intended to help people apply the law in practice. Guidance notes may include advice on action to be taken by employers in order to conform with the law.

- Both employers and employees have duties under the Health and Safety at Work, etc. Act 1974 (HSWA).

- The employer has a duty 'to ensure, as far as reasonably practicable, the health, safety and welfare at work of all his employees'. The employee has a duty to take reasonable care for the health and safety of himself and of other persons who may be affected by his acts or omissions at work.

- Every employer of five or more people must prepare and keep up to date a written statement of general policy with respect to the health and safety at work of employees, and the organization and arrangements for carrying out that policy, and to bring the statement and any revision of it to the notice of all employees.

- For all employers:
  - 'reasonably practicable' means that the degree of risk has to be balanced against the cost, time and difficulty of taking measures to avoid the risk;
  - 'practicable' means the cost, time and difficulty are not to be considered – technical feasibility is the only consideration;
  - 'absolute' – often indicated by the word 'shall' – means that the law must be obeyed.

- The Health and Safety Inspectorate have wide-reaching powers, including the right to enter and inspect any premises, at any time, where it is considered that there may be dangers to health or safety.

- A safety representative is someone appointed by a recognized trade union to represent employees on health and safety matters at work.

- An employer is legally obliged to set up a safety committee after receiving written requests to do so from two safety representatives.

# Session B
# The organization's responsibility for health, safety and the environment

## 1 Introduction

The Health and Safety at Work, etc. Act 1974 (HSWA) is a general enabling Act that allows Ministers to introduce more detailed Regulations and Approved Codes of Practice (ACOPS) relating to health and safety without taking every single one through Parliament.

It is not a statutory requirement for organizations to follow each ACOP, **but** the Courts will regard following them as evidence that an organization is abiding by the 'letter and the spirit' of HSWA and subsequent Regulations. Any organization that ignores ACOPs, where they exist, does so at its peril.

## 1.1 Your liability under the law

It is a sound principle of English law that ignorance is no defence.

This makes perfect sense, for without it, the speeding motorist, the burglar and the murderer would all claim that they 'didn't know they were doing anything wrong'. This principle also applies to all Health and Safety law, and this can be a frightening thought.

In practice, you cannot possibly remember every aspect of every part of the law. What you **must** do is to check for your own specific job and team responsibilities which aspects of the law may apply. For example, if your team works with display screens, then, either directly or through your manager, you need to check how the Regulations and/or ACOP will apply to their work.

The principle that 'ignorance is no defence' is not as onerous to apply as it may sound. It simply requires you to check how the law affects what you are doing specifically; it **doesn't** demand that you know everything about Health and Safety Law – there are few people indeed who could claim that knowledge.

These Regulations are sometimes referred to as the 'six pack'. They comprise:

- the Management of Health and Safety at Work Regulations 1999;
- the Workplace (Health, Safety and Welfare) Regulations 1992;
- the Manual Handling Operations Regulations 1992;
- the Health and Safety (Display Screen Equipment) Regulations 1992;
- the Personal Protective Equipment at Work Regulations 1992;
- the Provision and Use of Work Equipment Regulations 1998.

Another very significant piece of legislation is the Control of Substances Hazardous to Health Regulations (COSHH) 1999.

In this session we will review all these Regulations, and, in addition, look at the organization's responsibility for protecting the environment.

# 2 Management of Health and Safety at Work Regulations 1999 (MHSWR)

MHSWR applies to all kinds of work, apart from sea-going ships.

These regulations help to spell out the duties and responsibilities of employers much more explicitly than HSWA.

# 2.1 Main provisions of MHSWR

According to HSE:

'Their main provisions are designed to encourage a more systematic and better organized approach to dealing with health and safety.'

Specifically, MHSWR requires employers to:

1 **undertake 'suitable and sufficient' assessment of risks to health and safety**

MHSWR imposes a duty on employers to implement systematic risk assessments, which are recorded and updated whenever necessary.

The aim is to identify all significant risks in a workplace, to eliminate them wherever practicable and to minimize and control them where they cannot be eliminated.

Risk assessments must be recorded by all employers with more than five employees. They must be recorded in an accessible format, which may be paper-based or electronic.

In either case, the information must be accessible to HSE inspectors, safety representatives and other persons who have a right to gain access to the data.

2 **implement necessary measures**

Any required health and safety measures that follow from the risk assessment must then be put into practice.

EXTENSION 5
The approved code of practice, *Management of Health and Safety at Work Regulations, 1999* gives guidance on risk assessment.

## Comment

To carry out a **risk assessment**, you must:

- identify the hazard;
- measure and evaluate the risk from this hazard;
- put measures into place that will either eliminate the hazard, or control it.

## Example

In a work process involving the hand grinding of metal, one of the hazards is noise, and this fact must be recognized. During a risk assessment, the level of noise would need to be measured, and early action taken to protect workers – such as effective ear protectors.

For full coverage of risk assessment please refer to *Preventing Accidents* in this series.

3  provide health surveillance

Employers have to provide appropriate health surveillance for employees, where the risk assessment shows it to be necessary.

### Comment

The purpose of **health surveillance** is to:

■ identify adverse affects early, well before disease becomes obvious;
■ rectify inadequacies in control, and so reduce the risks to those affected or exposed;
■ inform those at risk, as soon as possible, of any damage to their health, so that they can take action, and perhaps change their job;
■ to reinforce health education, for example, by reminding workers to use the personal protective equipment provided.

Those whose health should be closely monitored include people who:

■ work in dust-laden atmospheres;
■ handle toxic or harmful substances, such as lead, chromium or pesticides;
■ work in noisy environments;
■ use equipment or materials potentially damaging to the eyes.

4  appoint competent persons

The Regulations counsel employers to appoint 'competent persons' to provide the Health and Safety assistance referred to in the Regulations. The ACOP does not tell employers what a competent person is under all circumstances, or where such people may be found. For example:

■ large employers may have an Occupational Health and Safety section, staffed with suitably qualified people
■ smaller organizations may appoint a specific person who has adequate knowledge and experience of their operations, or they may buy in the required expertise from an external consultant who also has sufficient understanding of their operations.

Whatever action an organization takes to satisfy the need for competent persons, the responsibility for health, safety and welfare remains with the organization itself. Ultimately, in practice, this means the person who signs the Health and Safety Policy Statement.

Increasing attention is being focused on the responsibilities of company directors for health and safety, following disasters such as major rail crashes.

MHSWR emphasizes that organizations cannot absolve their senior management of ultimate responsibility, no matter how many advisors they may have.

5   provide information

Employees, together with temporary employees and others in the employer's organization, must be given information they can understand about health and safety matters.

## 2.2 Malicious assaults on staff and equipment

Unfortunately, cases of assault by members of the general public have become more common in some workplaces, including hospitals, schools, shops and places of entertainment. Many such problems are likely to occur at odd times, outside normal working hours.

In circumstances where such assaults may occur, the employer should deal with it as another risk to be assessed and eliminated or minimized. For example, by:

- installing practicable security measures to protect staff while at the same time allowing normal work to continue;
- training staff in techniques that help them recognize and, wherever possible, defuse uncontrolled anger that may lead to assaults;
- providing emergency measures, such as panic buttons and alarms linked to the local police station, for staff to use if matters are getting out of hand;
- ensuring that first aid facilities and trained first aiders are available whenever they may be required.

Malicious behaviour may also threaten equipment or stock. The measures implemented to minimize risk also need to protect items such as alcohol, fuel, drugs and explosives (fireworks), taking account of the degree of risk which they may pose.

## Activity 13

**S/NVQ E6**

This Activity may provide the basis of appropriate evidence for your S/NVQ portfolio. If you are intending to take this course of action, it might be better to write your answers on separate sheets of paper.

As a team leader, you are expected to give information to your team members on their responsibilities for maintaining healthy, safe, and productive work conditions. This information should comply with your organization's requirements, and with the law.

Summarize the way that you currently go about fulfilling this responsibility.

_____

_____

_____

_____

_____

_____

Now write down the plans you have for improving the health and safety information you provide to your team.

_____

_____

_____

_____

_____

_____

Describe how you will ensure that they have understood this information.

_____

_____

_____

_____

_____

_____

To continue, MHSWR also requires employers to:

6    provide training

The Regulations impose detailed responsibilities for training, requiring employers to:

■ assess the capabilities of employees relative to particular tasks, for instance in handling loads manually;
■ provide induction training following recruitment;
■ give training whenever their work changes in a way that may expose them to new or increased risks, when, for example, they are required to work on equipment or processes new to them, or with alterations to established systems of working;

■ repeat training periodically as a refresher for established employees whenever necessary.

In effect, the regulations demand that employers carry out regular training needs analysis (TNA) and implement suitable training to meet the needs shown by the TNA.

# Activity 14

3 mins

The law imposes a duty on employers to provide any necessary training on safe practices. Make a note of at least **three** aspects of safe practice in which you think the law would expect training and information to be provided.

For example: 'how to work safely in a particular job'.

_____

_____

_____

_____

_____

_____

> Don't forget that, to your team, you represent the employer.

An employee needs to know, through clear instructions and/or training, everything that concerns personal safety, including:

■ how to work safely in his or her job;
■ what to do if something goes wrong;
■ where to find safety equipment, and how to use it;
■ all relevant legal requirements;
■ what steps he or she needs to take to safeguard the safety of others;
■ any special hazards.

MHSWR also requires employers to:

7   set up emergency procedures

8   co-operate with any other employers who share a work site

9   place duties on employees to follow health and safety instructions and report danger

10   consult employees' safety representatives and provide facilities for them.

Consultation must now take place on such matters as the:

- introduction of measures that may substantially affect health and safety;
- arrangements for appointing competent persons;
- health and safety information required by law;
- health and safety aspects of new technology being introduced to the workplace.

### To sum up

To repeat the main points included in MHSWR, employers must:

1 undertake 'suitable and sufficient' assessment of risks to health and safety;
2 implement necessary measures;
3 provide health surveillance;
4 appoint competent persons;
5 provide information;
6 provide training;
7 set up emergency procedures;
8 co-operate with any other employers who share a work site;
9 place duties on employees to follow health and safety instructions and report danger;
10 consult employees' safety representatives and provide facilities for them.

# Activity 15

3 mins

Make a note of the aspects of MHSWR you think you are most likely to be involved in, in your job as first line manager.

_____

_____

_____

_____

_____

_____

Managers at all levels may be expected to participate in implementing MHSWR. In particular, you may have noted:

- implementing specific measures, following risk assessment;
- providing information and training for your team;
- helping to set up emergency procedures.

# 3 Workplace (Health, Safety and Welfare) Regulations 1992 (WHSWR)

These Regulations replace a total of 38 items of older legislation. They cover many aspects of health, safety and welfare in the workplace, and apply to most places of work.

They do **not** apply to:

- ships and boats;
- building operations or works of engineering construction;
- mines and mineral exploration sites;
- work on agricultural or forestry land away from main buildings.

WHSWR stipulates general requirements for working conditions, related to:

**Are you obeying the law?**

As you read through these headings, tick the boxes of any subjects you feel are particularly relevant to your own circumstances, and that you would like to find out more about.

1   **the working environment** – including:

- ❏ temperature;
- ❏ ventilation;
- ❏ lighting;
- ❏ room dimensions;
- ❏ workstations and seating;
- ❏ outdoor workstations, such as weather protection.

### Example

The Regulations say that:

'Effective and suitable provision shall be made to ensure that every enclosed workspace is ventilated by a sufficient quantity of fresh or purified air.'

In offices and many other workplaces, windows will provide enough ventilation. Alternatively, air conditioning systems may be installed.

## Comment

Many of the requirements in these regulations appear to be 'common sense', and it is probably true to say that most workplaces are properly ventilated, heated and so on. Nevertheless, employers must obey the law.

2  **safety** – including:

- ❐ safe passage of pedestrians and vehicles;
- ❐ windows and skylights (safe opening, closing and cleaning);
- ❐ organization and control of traffic routes;
- ❐ glazed doors and partitions (use of safe material and marking);
- ❐ doors, gates and escalators (safety devices);
- ❐ floors (their construction and condition);
- ❐ obstructions and slipping and tripping hazards;
- ❐ falls from heights and into dangerous substances, and falling objects.

## Example

The Regulations say that:

1  'Every workplace shall be organized in such a way that pedestrians and vehicles can circulate in a safe manner.
2  Traffic routes in a workplace shall be suitable for the persons or vehicles using them, sufficient in number, in suitable positions and of sufficient size.'

The Code of Practice reminds us that: 'In some situations, people in wheelchairs may be at greater risk than people on foot, and special consideration should be given to their safety.'

3  **welfare facilities** – including:

- ❐ toilets;
- ❐ washing, eating and changing facilities;
- ❐ provision of drinking water;
- ❐ clothing storage, and facilities for changing clothing;
- ❐ seating;
- ❐ rest areas (and arrangements in them for non-smokers);
- ❐ rest facilities for pregnant women and nursing mothers.

## Example

The regulations say that:

'An adequate supply of drinking water shall be provided for all persons at work in the workplace.'

4 **housekeeping** – including:

❒ maintenance of workplace, equipment and facilities;
❒ cleanliness;
❒ removal of waste materials.

## Activity 16

The Regulations are very detailed and complex. However, you can make a note here if you want to find out more, and note the action you intend to take. (One way is to get hold of a copy of the Approved Code of Practice from the HSE, but you may be able to get the information through your organization. If you can get help with the interpretation of the Regulations, you should certainly do so.)

_____

_____

_____

_____

_____

_____

# 4 Manual Handling Operations Regulations 1992 (MHOR)

Accidents involving lifting and handling account for more than a third of all the accidents that cause people to be off work for more than three days, as reported through 'RIDDOR'. That averages more than 45,000 accidents per year over a five-year period, not including the less serious ones which don't get into the published statistics.

EXTENSION 6
The Manual Handling
Operations Regulations
1992 are explained in
the HSE booklet *Manual
Handing – Guidance on
Regulations.*

The MHOR Regulations cover the lifting and manoeuvring of loads of all types. They require the employer to:

■ consider whether a load must be moved, and, if so, whether it could be moved by non-manual methods;

■ assess the risk in manual operations and (unless it is very simple) make a written record of this assessment;

■ reduce the risk of injury as far as is reasonably practicable.

The following is a summary of the questions that should be asked regarding four aspects of a manual handling operation.[1]

## Making an assessment: some important questions

### 1 The task

■ Is the load held or manipulated at a distance from the trunk, so increasing the stress on the lower back?

■ Does the task involve:
– twisting the trunk?
– stooping?
– reaching upwards?
– excessive lifting or lowering distances?
– excessive carrying distances?

– pushing or pulling of the load?
– a risk of sudden movement of the load?
– frequent or prolonged physical effort?
– insufficient rest or recovery periods?
– a rate of work imposed by a process?

### 2 The load

■ Is the load:
– heavy?
– bulky or unwieldy?
– difficult to grasp?
– unstable, or are its contents likely to shift?
– sharp, hot or otherwise potentially damaging?

### 3 The working environment

■ Are there:
– space constraints preventing good posture?
– uneven, slippery or unstable floors?
– variations in the level of floors or work surfaces?
– extremes of temperature or humidity?
– ventilation problems or gusts of wind?
– poor lighting conditions?

[1] Adapted from *Manual Handling – Guidance on Regulations* published by HSE, pages 12–20.

### 4 Individual capability

- Does the task require unusual strength, height, etc.?
- Does the job put at risk those who might be pregnant or have a health problem?
- Does the task require special information or training for its safe performance?

## Activity 17

3 mins

|                                                                                      | Yes | No |
|--------------------------------------------------------------------------------------|-----|----|
| Does your team's job involve manual handling?                                        | ❑   | ❑  |
| Are you confident that you are managing manual handling tasks efficiently and effectively? | ❑   | ❑  |

If not, how will you learn more?

_____

_____

_____

Almost **every** job involves manual handling at some stage, and you don't have to be lifting heavy weights to become injured if you do it wrongly. It is for these reasons that the MHOR are so important to all managers, from legal, commercial and moral perspectives.

# 5 Health and Safety (Display Screen Equipment) Regulations 1992

EXTENSION 7
*VDUs: an easy guide to the Regulations. How to comply with the Health and Safety (display screen equipment) Regulations 1992.*

These Regulations put into law the employer's duties regarding the operation of display screen equipment by employees. Employers have to:

- assess and reduce the risks from display screen equipment;
- make sure that workstations satisfy minimum requirements;
- plan to allow breaks or change of activity;
- provide information and training for users;
- give users eye and eyesight tests and (if need be) special glasses.

Display screen equipment includes cathode ray tubes (CRTs), liquid crystal displays, and any other technology.

The Regulations do not apply to:

- drivers' cabs or control cabs for vehicles and machinery;
- display screen equipment on board a means of transport;
- display screen equipment mainly intended for public operation;
- portable systems not in prolonged use;
- calculators, cash registers or any equipment having a small data or measurement display required for direct use of the equipment;
- window typewriters.

The figure, and the text below it, summarize the minimum requirements for workstations.[2]

**Key to illustration:**

1   Adequate lighting

2   Adequate contrast, no glare or distracting reflections

3   Distracting noise minimized

4   Leg room and clearances to allow postural changes

5   Window covering

6   Software: appropriate to task adapted to user, provides feedback on system status, no undisclosed monitoring

7   Screen: stable image, adjustable, readable, glare/reflection free

8   Keyboard: usable, adjustable, detachable, legible

9   Work surface: allow flexible arrangements, spacious, glare free

10   Work chair: adjustable

11   Footrest

[2] Figure and text from *Display Screen Equipment Work – Guidance on Regulations* published by HSE.

Activity 18

3 mins

|  | Yes | No |
|---|---|---|
| Does your team's job involve working with display screen equipment for long periods? | ❏ | ❏ |
| Are you confident that you comply with the law? | ❏ | ❏ |

If not, how will you learn more?

_____

_____

_____

_____

# 6 Personal Protective Equipment at Work Regulations 1992 (PPEWR)

Personal protective equipment (PPE) includes eye, foot and head protection equipment, safety harnesses, life jackets, and so on. Employers have to:

- ensure that this equipment is suitable and appropriate;
- maintain, clean and replace it;
- provide storage for it when not in use;
- ensure that it is properly used;
- give employees training, information and instruction in its use.

It is illegal for an employer who provides PPE to make any charge to someone using it.

Complete the following Activity, to help you decide what further action you need to take regarding PPE.

# Activity 19

If your team needs to use personal protective equipment, or you think they may need to use it, answer the questions below.

- Is the equipment appropriate to the risks, and to the conditions at the place where exposure might occur? ❒

- Does it take account of ergonomic requirements, and the state of health of the persons who may wear it? ❒

- Does it fit the wearer? ❒

- Is it effective in preventing or controlling the risk? ❒

- Is it compatible with other equipment? ❒

- Have all the following risks been assessed?

| | | | |
|---|---|---|---|
| Head injury? | ❒ | Eye injury? | ❒ |
| Face injury? | ❒ | Inhalation of airborne contaminants? | ❒ |
| Noise-induced hearing loss? | ❒ | Skin contact? | ❒ |
| Bodily injury? | ❒ | Hand or arm injury? | ❒ |
| Leg or foot injury? | ❒ | Vibration-induced injury? | ❒ |

- Is appropriate accommodation provided for the PPE when it isn't in use? ❒

- Have the users been given adequate information, instruction and training? ❒

- Do all the users:

  - use the equipment in accordance with their training and instructions? ❒

  - return the PPE to its accommodation after use? ❒

  - understand the need to report losses or defects? ❒

What further actions do you intend to take about PPE?

_____

_____

_____

_____

_____

_____

**S/NVQ E6**

# 7 Provision and Use of Work Equipment Regulations 1998 (PUWER)

The definition of 'work equipment' is very wide, and includes a butcher's knife, a combine harvester and even a complete power station. Employers must:

- take into account working conditions and hazards when selecting equipment;
- ensure equipment is suitable for use, and is properly maintained;
- provide adequate instruction, information and training.

The next Activity is a very brief summary checklist. Complete it to help you decide what action you might want to take in regard to work equipment.

## Activity 20

**S/NVQ E6**

Identify an important item of equipment that your team works with. Then answer the following questions about it.

Item: _____

- Is the equipment suitable for the use it is put to?                                    ❐
- Is it well and regularly maintained?                                                   ❐
- Are adequate information and instructions available to potential users?   ❐
- Have the users received adequate training in its use?                          ❐
- Have you provided protection against dangerous parts of the
  equipment, such as guards around rotating parts?                               ❐
- Have measures been taken to eliminate or control risks associated
  with the use of the equipment?                                                        ❐
- Are stop controls provided that are easy to reach, and well marked?    ❐
- Are control systems (if any) safe?                                                     ❐
- Is isolation provided from sources of energy?                                       ❐

- Is the equipment stable? ☐

- Is it well lit, and marked with appropriate signs and warnings? ☐

Do you need to find out more about the use of work equipment, or these Regulations? Write down any actions you intend to take.

_____

_____

_____

_____

_____

_____

So much for the six Regulations that form the 'six pack'. Now we will look at another very important set of Regulations.

# 8 Control of Substances Hazardous to Health Regulations 1994 (COSHH)

> COSHH doesn't cover asbestos, lead, materials producing ionizing radiation and substances below ground in mines, which all have their own legislation.

The Control of Substances Hazardous to Health Regulations (COSHH) potentially affect any substance used for any purpose in the workplace. Even food ingredients can be hazardous in some circumstances. Sugar can be involved in dust explosions and flour can be implicated in occupational asthma.

The Regulations require users to carry out risk assessments on every **potentially** hazardous substance and to take appropriate action when the assessment has been made.

# Activity 21 · 3 mins

Can you think of any substances which could possibly affect the health of people where you work?

_____

_____

_____

_____

_____

_____

_____

_____

There are over 40,000 substances which are classed as hazardous. Wherever you work – in a food factory, a shop, a garage, a warehouse, a laboratory, an engineering works, a hospital, a farm, a garden centre or an office – hazardous substances will probably be present. They may include:

- anything brought into a workplace to be worked on, used or stored, including corrosives, acids or solvents used in cleaning materials;
- dust and fumes given off by a work process;
- finished products or residues from a work process.

Example of label

Toxic or very toxic

Anything very toxic, toxic, corrosive, harmful or irritant comes under COSHH. Examples are chemicals, agricultural pesticides, wood treatment chemicals, dusts and substances containing harmful micro-organisms. By law, the containers of hazardous substances must be labelled as being hazardous, and they must state what the hazard is.

Assessing the hazards of substances and the potential harm if they are mixed with **other** substances is a highly technical subject. The law recognizes this and requires specialist manufacturers and suppliers of substances to provide comprehensive information to users (usually in the form of data sheets) to help guard them against risks which they may not have the technical knowledge to anticipate. Manufacturers will also provide further data on request as a part of their obligations under COSHH.

Activity 22

15 mins

EXTENSION 8
is a model data sheet
which might be used by
the manufacturer of a
chemical product.

Find an example of a data sheet relating to a hazardous substance in your own department or organisation. Then make sure that you know where the data sheets are kept for all hazardous substances with which you might come into contact.

## 8.1 Employers' duties under COSHH

Under the COSHH Regulations, employers have to:

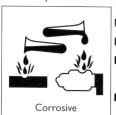

Example of label

Corrosive

- **determine the hazard** of substances used by the organization;
- **assess the risk** to people's health from the way the substances are used;
- **prevent anyone being exposed** to the substances, if possible;
- if exposure cannot be prevented, decide how to **control the exposure** so as to **reduce the risk**, and then establish effective controls;
- ensure that the controls are **properly used and maintained**;
- **examine and test the control measures**, if this is required;
- **inform, instruct and train** employees (and non-employees on the premises), so that they are aware of the hazards and how to work safely;
- if necessary, **monitor the exposure** of employees (and non-employees on the premises), and provide **health surveillance** to employees if necessary.

## 8.2 Your job and COSHH

Now let us consider what impact COSHH has on your job.

# Activity 23 ·  5 mins

From what you've read so far, can you suggest how first line managers and team leaders can play a part in helping their employer comply with the COSHH Regulations, and so reduce the risk to employees from hazardous substances? Try to list **two** or **three** positive actions that might be taken by someone in your position.

_____

_____

_____

Example of label

Harmful or irritant

■ Probably the most important role first-line managers and team leaders can play is in informing and training the workteam about the hazards and the correct procedures to be followed. We'll look at the kind of information and training needed in a moment.

■ They can and should ensure that safety procedures are followed, and set a personal example in following the correct procedures consistently and carefully.

■ Team leaders are also usually in a good position to assess the likely behaviour of people when they have to deal with hazardous situations. If so, they can assist their employer in determining what people do and what they might do.

■ If protective clothing and/or emergency facilities are provided, it is often the team leader's job to ensure that these items are available when they're needed, and are properly maintained.

■ Leaders should ensure that the only substances used are those whose risks have been assessed, and that team members have been trained in the safe handling of these substances.

Let's now look at the aspects of training and providing information to staff about hazardous substances.

A team leader will need to make sure of the following.

■ Team members should understand the hazards.

All suppliers are compelled by law to label hazardous substances. Everyone using such a substance needs to be trained to read and understand container labels and to follow the supplier's advice.

■ Team members should understand how risks are controlled.

Procedures for controlling risks must be clearly laid down.

■ Team members should understand the precautions they have to take.

Precautions and procedures will almost certainly need to be demonstrated.

■ Team members should understand what to do in the case of an emergency.

Emergency procedures need to be demonstrated and practised.

■ Team members should always feel able to ask for guidance.

There should be an atmosphere of trust so that if people are not sure of the right course of action in particular circumstances, they feel free to ask for help or advice from their manager, specialist advisors, or the manufacturer.

# Activity 24

**S/NVQ E6**

This Activity may provide the basis of appropriate evidence for your S/NVQ portfolio. If you are intending to take this course of action, it might be better to write your answers on separate sheets of paper.

There are few workplaces where hazardous substances do not exist. If you have hazardous substances in your work area, what training does your team receive about them? Summarize the kind of training they get.

_____

_____

_____

_____

_____

_____

Based on the points listed above, write down your plans for improving their training in this important area.

_____

_____

_____

_____

_____

_____

What further actions do you think you need to take, in order to comply with COSHH? (You may decide to find out more about the Regulations before you answer this.)

_____

_____

_____

_____

_____

_____

Now we have covered the 'six-pack' Regulations, and looked at COSHH, we move on to some other important health and safety laws.

# 9 Environmental responsibilities

As well as its responsibilities for the health and safety of employees, visitors and the general public, employers also have responsibility for ensuring that their activities do not cause any harm to the environment. In recent years this responsibility has been heightened by growing concerns about the effect of emissions of carbon dioxide on the climate. However, environmental concerns have been growing for many years because of the potential effects on the health of the public of industrial and other types of activity.

Regulations now exist covering many aspects of these activities, most derived from the Environmental Protection Act 1990, which consolidated many existing laws relating to the environment and extended controls over a wide range of activities that have a significant impact on it. Organizations must obtain permits to undertake these activities, and must show that they are using the Best Available Techniques (BAT) to minimize their environmental impact. There is also a 'duty of care' on all those involved in collecting, disposing or treating waste, and its import and export. The EPA also extended the Clean Air Acts to control nuisances (e.g. unpleasant odours) and added controls over litter, genetically modified organisms, and the supply, storage and use of polluting substances.

## 9.1 Air pollution

The Environmental Protection Act 1990 contains the main legislation about nuisance in England, Wales and Scotland and is enforced by the local authorities.

The Public Health (Ireland) Act 1878 contains the main legislation relating to statutory nuisances in Northern Ireland. Under Part III of The Pollution Control and Local Government (Northern Ireland) Order 1978, district councils have powers to deal with noise nuisance.

A nuisance is anything that could be 'prejudicial to people's health or interfere with a person's legitimate use and enjoyment of land', particularly to any neighbours in their homes and gardens. A nuisance could arise from the poor state of premises or from noise, smoke, fumes, gases, dust, steam, smell, and, in England and Wales, insects and artificial lighting.

# 9.2 Energy

The UK Government is committed to a target of reducing greenhouse gas emissions by 12.5% by 2008–2012, based on 1990 levels. It has encouraged businesses to use fossil fuels more efficiently and reduce emissions of greenhouse gases, particularly carbon dioxide. This is reinforced by the Climate Change Levy, which is a tax on the use of energy by industry, commerce, agriculture and the public sector, paid through energy bills since April 2001.

Major energy consuming businesses receive allowances for their permitted Carbon Dioxide emissions. If they reduce their emissions below this level they can sell their allowance, through what is known as the emissions trading scheme, enabling other organisations to exceed their allowance.

# 9.3 Hazardous substances

Although the use of many hazardous substances is controlled through COSHH, there are also regulations about the storage, transporting and processing of a number of hazardous substances which could pollute the environment if not properly controlled. This includes:

- Animal by-products;
- Hazardous or special waste (e.g. the disposal of toxic waste materials);
- Oil storage;
- Ozone depleting substances (most of which are being phased out);
- Pesticides and biocides;
- Radioactive substances and wastes;
- Restriction of hazardous substances in electrical and electronic equipment (RoHS).

# 9.4 Land

Industrial processes that have been undertaken for years on the same site can lead to contamination, which is a hazard to the environment and human health. Generally speaking, the organization responsible for the contamination will also be responsible for clearing it, which can prove to be very expensive, so potential contaminating processes should be well protected. Prevention may be expensive, but could be even more expensive later if not done!

There are also regulations on operating a landfill site and producers of waste that is sent to landfill – an organization is responsible for ensuring that waste that is sent for landfill is disposed of properly and not illegally dumped.

# 9.5 Packaging

A business that handles more than 50 tonnes of packaging a year and has a turnover of more than £2 million must comply with the Producer Responsibility Obligations and register with the environmental regulator (the Environment Agency in England and Wales, the Environment and Heritage Service in Northern Ireland and the Scottish Environmental Protection Agency in Scotland). They must also comply with the Essential Requirements Regulations which mean that they must:

- minimize the packaging used;
- ensure packaging can be reused or recycled;
- ensure packaging does not contain high levels of certain heavy metals.

# 9.6 Permits and licenses

A wide variety of activities now require special permits or licenses. These include:

- the disposal of 'end-of-life' vehicles (which manufacturers now must take responsibility for);
- landfill;
- Pollution Prevention and Control permits for most industrial processes;
- handling radioactive substances and wastes;
- discharges of trade effluent to sewers;
- registration of waste carriers, brokers and dealers;
- waste incineration and waste management licences;
- water abstraction and pollution.

## 9.7 Business efficiency

As controls on environmental harm are increased and as the costs associated with the use of materials and energy and the disposal of waste increase, so it becomes increasingly important for organizations to look for ways of improving the way they use energy, reduce the amout of waste they produce and limit any harmful emissions into the atmosphere. The combination of taxes (like the Climate Change Levy), charges for permits and licences, and restrictions on certain activities are all designed to make it more attractive to organizations to minimise their use of energy and the production of waste.

Activity 25    2 mins

Review your organization's activities and, in particular, those over which you have responsibility.

■  What aspects of its operations may have a potential impact on the environment?
■  Is any aspect of these activities controlled by permits or licences and, if so, what are the specific requirements relating to these?
■  What, if anything, is done to control energy use and the production of waste?
■  How effective is this, and what could be done to reduce waste, reuse or recycle materials and avoid causing harm to the environment?

_____

_____

_____

_____

_____

_____

_____

_____

_____

_____

_____

# Self-assessment 2

20 mins

1　Match each requirement under the Management of Health and Safety at Work Regulations, (MHSWR) on the left with the correct comment on the right.

**Under MHSWR, employers must:**　**This includes the process of:**

a　provide risk assessment

b　provide health surveillance

c　appoint competent persons

d　consult employees' safety representatives

i　identifying adverse affects; rectifying inadequacies in control; informing those at risk of any damage to their health; reinforcing health education

ii　identifying measures that may substantially affect health and safety; identifying health and safety aspects of new technology; discussing these with the relevant people

iii　identifying the hazard; measuring and evaluating the risk from this hazard; putting measures into place that will either eliminate the hazard, or control it

iv　identifying those with sufficient training, and experience or knowledge and other qualities; requiring them to devise and apply the measures needed to comply with health and safety laws.

2　For each activity on the left, identify **one** regulation that will apply to it, taken from the list on the right.

**Activity**

i　Loading bags of flour

_____

ii　Supervising telesales

_____

iii　Running an electrical department in a superstore

_____

iv　Training fork-lift truck drivers in a fuel depot

_____

v　Supervising an area where there are high levels of dust

_____

vi　Supervising on a building site

**Regulation**

a　Management of Health and Safety at Work Regulations (MHSWR)

b　Workplace (Health, Safety and Welfare) Regulations (WHSWR)

c　Manual Handling Operations Regulations (MHOR)

d　Health and Safety (Display Screen Equipment) Regulations

e　Personal Protective Equipment at Work (PPE) Regulations (PPEWR)

3 Fill in the blanks in the following statements with suitable words taken from the list below.

CONTROL          INSTRUCT          SAFELY
CONTROLS         MAINTAINED        SUBSTANCES
EXPOSED          MONITOR           SURVEILLANCE
HAZARD           RISK              TEST
HEALTH

Under the COSHH Regulations, employers have to:

■ determine the _____ of _____ used by the organization;

■ assess the _____ to people's health from the way the substances are used;

■ prevent anyone being _____ to the substances, if possible;

■ if exposure cannot be prevented, decide how to _____ the exposure so as to reduce the risk, and then establish effective _____;

■ ensure that the controls are properly used and _____;

■ examine and _____ the control measures, if this is required;

■ inform, _____ and train employees (and non-employees on the premises), so that they are aware of the hazards and how to work _____;

■ if necessary, _____ the exposure of employees (and non-employees on the premises), and provide _____ _____ to employees if necessary.

4 Businesses must register with the environmental regulator and comply with the Producer Responsibility Obligations if they:

■ handle more than _____ of packaging;

■ have a turnover of more than £ _____.

Answers to these questions can be found on pages 177.

# 10 Summary

- The Management of Health and Safety at Work Regulations 1999 (MHSWR) are designed to encourage a more systematic and better organized approach to dealing with health and safety.

- Under MHSWR, employers must:
  - assess the risks of the job;
  - implement necessary measures;
  - provide health surveillance;
  - appoint competent persons;
  - provide information and training;
  - set up emergency procedures;
  - co-operate with any other employers who share a work site;
  - place duties on employees to follow health and safety instructions and report danger;
  - consult employees' safety representatives and provide facilities for them.

- The Workplace (Health, Safety and Welfare) Regulations 1992 (WHSWR) stipulates general requirements for working conditions, related to:
  - the working environment;
  - safety;
  - welfare facilities;
  - housekeeping.

- The Manual Handling Operations Regulations 1992 (MHOR) require the employer to:
  - consider whether a load must be moved, and if so, whether it could be moved by non-manual methods;
  - assess the risk in manual operations and (unless it is very simple) make a written record of this assessment;
  - reduce the risk of injury as far as is reasonably practicable.

- The Health and Safety (Display Screen Equipment) Regulations 1992 require employers to:
  - assess and reduce the risks from display screen equipment;
  - make sure that workstations satisfy minimum requirements;
  - plan to allow breaks or change of activity;
  - provide information and training for users;
  - give users eye and eyesight tests and (if need be) special glasses.

- The Personal Protective Equipment at Work (PPE) Regulations 1992 (PPEWR) require employers to:
  - ensure PPE equipment is suitable and appropriate;
  - maintain, clean and replace it;
  - provide storage for it when not in use;
  - ensure that it is properly used;
  - give employees training, information and instruction in its use.

- The Provision and Use of Work Equipment Regulations 1998 (PUWER) require employers to:

  - take into account working conditions and hazards when selecting equipment;
  - ensure equipment is suitable for use, and is properly maintained;
  - provide adequate instruction, information and training.

- Under the Control of Substances Hazardous to Health Regulations, 1999 (COSHH) regulations, employers have to:

  - determine the hazard of substances used by the organization;
  - assess the risk to people's health from the way the substances are used;
  - prevent anyone being exposed to the substances, if possible;
  - if exposure cannot be prevented, decide how to control the exposure so as to reduce the risk, and then establish effective controls;
  - ensure that the controls are properly used and maintained;
  - examine and test the control measures, if this is required;
  - inform, instruct and train employees (and non-employees on the premises), so that they are aware of the hazards and how to work safely;
  - if necessary, monitor the exposure of employees (and non-employees on the premises), and provide health surveillance to employees if necessary.

- The Environmental Protection Act 1990 and related regulations control:

  - air pollution;
  - energy use;
  - hazardous substances;
  - land use;
  - packaging;
  - waste management and disposal.

# Session C
# Accidents and their causes

## 1 Introduction

Accidents happen everywhere: in the home, on the road, in sporting events; the world has never been a completely safe place. But we expect a place of work to be a controlled environment, where everyone has a defined role to play, and which operates according to a set of rules. Here, if anywhere, the actions of people, and events, should be regulated and well-organized. And yet, alas, accidents at work continue to cost hundreds of lives each year, and thousands of injuries.

On average, **six** people are killed at work **every week** in this country.

This fact can't only be explained by lack of resources: tough bosses thinking only of profits, rather than the safety and welfare of their employees. In many industries, organizations invest enormous sums in making workplaces safe and healthy. Go into any large chemical works, for example, and see the systems, the precautions, the continuous training programmes; you will hear and read the words 'safe' and 'safety' many times during a day. But accidents **still** happen, even in the best-run workplaces. Many occur because people, for some reason, neglect to take simple precautions; others come about as a result of poor supervision. Whatever the cause, it must concern management, for it is managers at all levels who have the task of implementing systems of safety, and of ensuring they are maintained.

It is a fact that accidents happen in all working environments and not just in large-scale manufacturing plants. The construction industries and agriculture both have records significantly worse than average, and many accidents happen in offices, shops and other premises, such as holiday venues, into which the public are invited.

We begin this session by defining what we mean by an accident. Then we'll list a number of 'classic' accidents, and look at some examples.

Next, we'll start to examine causes, in order to help us formulate some ideas for preventing accidents.

# 2 Definition of an accident

'Fatal accident', 'happened accidentally', 'happy accident' – when we use the word 'accident' we wrap up a lot of assumptions about chance, disaster and responsibility, or lack of it. So what **do** we mean by an 'accident'?

## Activity 26

3 mins

What is an accident? Try to define it, in your own words.

_____

_____

_____

_____

_____

_____

There are many ways of explaining the word 'accident', but most people would think of an accident as something that:

- occurs by chance, rather than by design;
- is unwanted, unplanned and unexpected;
- perhaps involves harm or injury to someone;
- often results in interruptions to normal activities, including work;
- perhaps results in damage to physical things, or to the environment.

One definition of an accident is given by the Health and Safety Executive:

Accident includes any undesired circumstances which give rise to:

- ill health or injury;
- damage to property, plant, products or the environment;
- production losses or increased liabilities.[1]

However, it is unwise to ignore incidents which **do not** result in harm, damage or business loss. If you are driving in a line of traffic that suddenly comes to a stop, and you narrowly avoid hitting the car in front, it may make you realize that you aren't leaving yourself sufficient stopping distance. In the same way, the Civil Aviation Authority investigate 'near misses' involving aircraft because they know that doing so will help to prevent serious accidents.

Two other words that we will use in this workbook are 'hazard' and 'risk'.

- **Hazard** means **the potential to cause harm**, including:
  - ill health and injury;
  - damage to property, plant, products or the environment;
  - production losses or increased liabilities.

- **Risk** means **the likelihood that a specified undesired event will occur** due to the realization of a hazard:
  - by, or during, work activities; or
  - by the products and services created by work activities.

So, hazard is the **potential** to cause harm, damage or business loss. Risk is the **likelihood** that the potential harm from a hazard will be realized.

## Activity 27

3 mins

One more definition: how would you explain the word **danger?**

_____

_____

_____

_____

[1] This definition, together with those for 'hazard' and 'risk', is adapted from _Successful Health and Safety Management_, published by HSE Books, Crown copyright, 1991.

**Danger** can be described as:

- **an unacceptable level of risk**; or
- **liability or exposure to harm**; or
- **something that causes peril**.

**Safety** is the result of the activities we carry out to **keep something or somebody from harm**, and could be called the opposite of danger.

We achieve safety by protecting ourselves and our environment, and by identifying, assessing, and then reducing or eliminating, the risk from the hazards we may encounter.

This workbook is mostly concerned with recognizing hazards and preventing accidents. We start with the assumption that:

**most accidents are preventable**

through applying proper risk management techniques and using fully the best technical information available.

# 3 What kind of accidents?

EXTENSION 9
This book is listed on page 175. This list is adapted from *Classic Accidents*.

In his book *Classic Accidents*, David Farmer list seven 'classic' accident types. These are not the only kind of accident, but are ones that occur repeatedly, in workplaces everywhere. As David Farmer says: 'They keep on happening to different people, at different times, and in different places.' The seven classics are:

- people getting caught in machinery by their hair, or by something they are wearing;
- people falling when using ladders;
- collisions involving reversing vehicles;
- people being burned when using or handling flammable liquids, usually as a result of being ignorant of the hazards;
- people in confined spaces, sometimes together with their rescuers, being overcome by gassing or asphyxiation;
- accidents by tripping, slipping, or falling;
- accidents during maintenance work.

Falls from height account for around 25% of all fatal accidents every year. Falls from as little as 2 metres not infrequently cause death!

Let's look at some cases.

## Entanglements in machinery

A young man was using a portable electric drill fitted with an abrasive disc to clean some metalwork. As he leaned over the work, his tie became entangled and wrapped itself around the drill chuck. Before he could stop the drill, it had wound itself around the tie, and travelled upwards. The abrasive disc caused the young man severe facial injuries.

Entanglement accidents often start with a strand of hair, or a loose item of clothing, which becomes caught up. The victim is usually unable to draw back before a finger, a limb, or the whole body, becomes enmeshed.

A woman using a bench-mounted drill moved her hand across the bench to clear it of clutter. The drill bit caught in her wedding ring, and severely damaged the flesh and tendons of her finger, which surgeons later had to amputate.

## Ladder accidents

A man slipped while climbing a short ladder, which was resting on a scaffold tower. Neither ladder nor tower was properly secured, and the tower fell over. The man's head hit a concrete path, injuring him fatally.

Ladders, though useful, are not inherently safe. Even when the ladder is securely fixed, so that it cannot move from side to side, it is still easy for the user to slip on the rungs.

A decorator was climbing a wooden ladder carrying an open pot of paint. His shoes were wet, and one foot slipped on a rung. While he was struggling to regain his balance, the paint splashed over his face and eyes, temporarily blinding him. He again lost his footing and fell, breaking both legs.

## Reversing vehicle accidents

A delivery lorry, reversing in a school car-park, collided with a car driven by a parent, and rammed it against a wall. Although the lorry was fitted with an automatic reversing horn, the car-driver failed to hear it over the noise of her radio. She was trapped in the vehicle for about an hour, and received severe leg lacerations.

Visibility from the cab of a reversing lorry is typically poor. Warning devices help, but there is no real substitute for a trained banksman on the ground, telling the driver what to do.

A refuse collection vehicle was reversing outside a hospital, when it hit an outpatient, killing him outright.

## Flammable liquid accidents

In a hospital surgical unit, a theatre nurse spilled some ether on her uniform. A short while later, a spark was formed from the static electricity generated by her underclothes, which were made from a synthetic material. As a result, the ether-impregnated uniform caught fire, and she was badly burned.

A man took the bung out of a drum that had been standing around for four years, and applied an oxy-acetylene torch to the drum, with the intention of removing the top. Flammable gases had been accumulating inside the drum, and the torch caused an explosion.

## Accidents in a confined space

A farm labourer was asphyxiated while trying to unblock an underground slurry reception tank. The farmer, in his efforts to rescue his employee, was also overcome. Both men died. Slurry gives off gases that drive out oxygen; the men in the tank were simply unable to breathe.

A brewery worker was cleaning the inside of a large copper vessel. Unable to remove some stubborn stains, he decided, without reference to anyone else, to apply nitric acid. Later, he became ill, and was taken to hospital. Doctors were initially given incorrect information about the work he had been doing by the brewery management, who assumed the worker had been using the recommended materials, which would be either a mild alkali solution or a paste made from pumice and tartaric acid. When it was discovered he was suffering from the effects of nitrous fumes, the man was treated appropriately, and fortunately recovered.

## Tripping, falling, or slipping accidents

A twenty-year old packer went to the tea-room for her midday refreshment, where boiling water for making tea was kept in a freestanding electrical boiler. She slipped on the wet floor, instinctively grabbed the boiler for support and pulled it over on top of her. She received extensive burns. The water on the floor had come from the boiler, which had a dripping tap.

A woman visitor was walking in the grounds of a sports centre, carrying some equipment. As she walked over a 'sleeping policeman' ramp in the road, the heel of her shoe caught in a circular slot used to carry a fixing bolt. She fell so badly on one arm that a smashed bone had to be removed from her elbow.

> Slips, trips, and falls account for around twenty per cent of all accidents at work in the UK. Injuries are often serious, and occasionally fatal.

## Accidents during maintenance

A young worker was cleaning inside a mixing vessel, at the bottom of which were rotating blades. The interlock system was faulty, and the vessel was powered up while the worker was still inside. The young man lost both his feet, which were cut off at the ankles.

> About a quarter of fatal accidents take place during maintenance operations on buildings or equipment. As this kind of work is usually carried out infrequently, workers are not always familiar with the hazards.

A self-employed contractor arrived early one morning to start work repairing a school roof. Impatient for his colleagues to arrive, he started to inspect the work to be done, by climbing on, and walking along, the roof. He slipped and fell through a skylight, cutting himself badly.

How can accidents like these be prevented? Before we look at specific accident types, we'll consider the subject in broader terms.

 # 4 What causes accidents?

The 'classic' accident cases we have just looked at were all preventable, but apparently all had different causes. It would be possible, no doubt, to describe fifty or a hundred other work accidents, and each might seem to have come about through a unique set of circumstances.

So how can we talk about 'accident prevention' in any general manner?

# Activity 28

3 mins

Can you think of **one** feature that **all** work accidents have in common? If you're stuck for an answer look back to the incidents above. Ignore the particular sequences of events that might have led to each accident – and think about **people** and **organizations.**

_____

_____

_____

_____

The 'technical' causes of different accidents may have nothing in common. So to find a common feature we need to move away from technicalities and think in more general terms.

Your response to this Activity may have been to note one of the following:

- poor supervision;
- inadequate training;
- lack of instruction;
- lack of information;
- inadequate procedures.

These would all be correct. The **majority** of accidents result from these kinds of failures.

Although an accident is always unexpected, when we look back we often realize that it should have come as no surprise. Something happens that should never have been allowed to happen. In other words, safety procedures and controls are inadequate.

So perhaps the best response to this Activity might be:

**accidents at work are largely caused by poor control and management of safety.**

As The Health and Safety Executive (HSE) puts it:

'The majority of accidents and incidents are not caused by "careless workers", but by failures in control (either within the organization or within a particular job), which are the responsibility of management.'[2]

Safety at work can only be achieved if there are well-organized **systems** of safety. The reasons are that:

- the safety of people at work depends on co-operation between individuals and between groups;
- people at work largely do what they are told to do or what they are allowed to do;
- people at work tend to assume that someone higher in the organization is making sure that the workplace is safe.

Such a system is a definite policy or strategy for safety, and a set of clear procedures and rules. It takes into account the fact that people are human, are not all equally well-equipped to cope, and may make mistakes. A good system looks at the way people work, and encourages them to be aware of the hazards. When accidents occur, it's usually either because the safety system is inadequate, or because somebody has bypassed the system.

So we can look at reasons why accidents happen from two viewpoints: the circumstances leading up to particular accidents, that is, the technical causes, and the system that allowed them to take place. We can think about accidents on the road from these points of view. The road traffic safety system comprises (at least):

- the state and design of the roads, and programmes of road maintenance;
- the highway code, which sets out the rules of driving;
- the driving test, which is designed to ensure that all drivers reach a minimum standard;
- the drivers themselves;
- the quality of vehicles;
- the policing of roads.

Most road traffic accidents are caused by people doing foolish things (and so bypassing the system), or as a result of mechanical failure. It may be possible to analyse why a particular accident took place, and so do a lot to stop it happening again. But if we want to get the overall accident rate down, we may have to improve the system. (Better roads? Better cars? More stringent policing? Lower speed limits? Different attitudes?)

---

[2] Taken from *Successful Health and Safety Management*, Health and Safety Executive, Crown copyright, 1991.

Later in this session, we will discuss some of the key elements needed for a successful health and safety management system at work.

Let's first look at another couple of accidents and see if we can analyse the causes behind them.

# 4.1 Who's responsible?

A common first reaction to an accident is to look for someone to blame.

Activity 29 · 5 mins

Helen Ripon worked for a small company on a trading estate, employing 20 staff. It acted as an agency for a number of publishers of technical manuals, storing their books, taking orders and despatching them to customers.

There had been lots of arguments about tea and coffee making. The firm refused to supply a machine, on the grounds of cost and complications with VAT and said staff must 'use the cafe on the estate'.

Helen brought in a kettle from home and organized a 'coffee club' amongst the staff. The Manager, though aware of what she was doing, said nothing about it.

The kettle was an old one and the connector on its lead had been mended with insulating tape. One morning, the cleaner, not a member of the 'club', decided to make himself a cup of tea. He received an electrical shock from the faulty connector, was seriously hurt and rushed to hospital.

1     What were the circumstances that led up to this accident, the technical causes?

2     Who was responsible for the accident? Tick which of the following you think were responsible and say briefly why this was the case:

Helen                                                       ❒

_____

_____

the cleaner                                          ❒

_____

_____

the manager                                         ❒

_____

_____

senior management                                 ❒

_____

_____

the safety officer, advisor or manager – had there been one     ❒

_____

_____

the kettle's maker                                    ❒

_____

_____

You'll probably find that the technical cause was very simple:

■     the kettle had a faulty connector;
■     it had been mended in a way which was inherently unsafe.

Who was responsible?

■     Helen was responsible.

She had brought unauthorized equipment onto site, which she knew had a fault which had not been mended safely.

- The cleaner had some responsibility.

  He was not authorized to use any equipment other than that required for cleaning.

- The manager was responsible.

  He had turned a 'blind eye' to the use of unauthorized equipment which had not been tested in the way required by law for all 'portable electrical equipment' used on the site.

- Senior management bore some responsibility.

  They had allowed a situation to develop which had led to a serious accident by failing to resolve a simple problem and failing to enforce their own safety policies.

- The Safety Officer, Manager or Advisor – was not responsible.

  If there was such a person, the role is an advisory one. It would be unreasonable to expect such a person to monitor every faulty condition or working practice which might exist.

  The kettle's maker was not responsible.

- Clearly, the kettle was being used with an obvious fault that was not a 'design fault' and had been mended in a way which the manufacturer would not have approved.

  Many accidents, including **serious** ones, result from simple causes which any reasonable employee or manager could understand and predict.

  This simple, but potentially fatal accident, was the responsibility of several people and probably would not have happened **if only** one of them had acted more responsibly.

## 4.2 What went wrong?

If something serious happens, it is essential from a legal and moral standpoint to investigate.

- Small firms like the one Helen worked for, have a far worse accident record than larger ones doing the same work – which is all the more reason for them to investigate accidents systematically.

  Here's a description of another incident.

# Activity 30 ·

5 mins

Eighteen-year-old Karen began work at an in-store bakery for a local supermarket on a busy market day. The section leader was delighted to see her as they were short-handed, telling her that she would get 'proper induction' tomorrow, when it was quieter. She was issued with overalls and told that safety footwear would be issued during induction.

She was set to work emptying trays from one of the large mobile racks used to move baked products into the selling area.

The first rack proved no problem and she moved on to the second one. The first tray she picked up proved to be extremely hot and had sharp corners. It cut and burned both of her hands quite badly. She reeled back, and in doing so dragged the tray out of the rack. It fell on her left foot, bruising the toes. Her training shoes gave little protection.

Imagine you were asked to investigate this accident. Jot down at least three questions which you might ask.

Some of the questions you might have asked are listed here:

- Why was Karen set to work before she had been given any induction training?
- Was she warned that bakery items, like racks and trays, do not **look** hot, being black in colour, but often may have come straight out of an oven?
- Why was she not told to use protective oven gloves every time she handled all potentially hot items?
- Were other people not wearing protective footwear?
- Did the Section Leader's **Manager** condone the practice of starting people before any safety induction – was it 'custom and practice' to do so?
- Had any risk assessments been done for working around ovens? If so, were there any written procedures and/or local warning signs?
- Had other employees suffered similar injuries?

You may well have asked other questions. Accident investigations frequently show that more than one factor led to the problem:

- the acts of, or failure to act by, people is a common factor in most accidents;
- complicated 'technical' matters are not involved in the vast majority of accidents.

'If only' is a phrase often heard after an accident.

In the incidents described in the two Activities, the hazards (electric shock from a faulty lead and extreme heat in and around ovens) seem perfectly obvious. But:

- so is driving a car at sixty miles an hour on a foggy motorway – many people do that, as the accident figures prove;
- too often, people assume that it 'won't happen to me' – until it does.

In the second incident, Karen was both young and new to the job. She belonged to two of the most vulnerable groups of employees.

**Accident statistics show over many years that young people, new starters and older workers suffer a relatively high number of accidents.**

Karen belonged to two of these categories and should have been treated accordingly.

It isn't possible to eliminate every hazard from the workplace. But where the hazards are known, it is morally and legally imperative to protect people from them, paying particular attention to the most vulnerable groups.

# 5 Policies for safety

So what is the best management approach to accident prevention?

Those organizations that have succeeded in improving their safety records have found that a successful approach to safety entails:

- issuing a clear **health and safety policy** that everyone knows and understands;
- establishing safety **objectives** that are realistic and achievable;
- providing **resources** to make the objectives achievable;
- setting safety **standards** that are measurable, and against which the objectives can be compared;

- **identifying hazards** and **assessing the risks** from them;
- putting systems in place that **eliminate the hazards** or **reduce the risks**;
- setting up procedures for **monitoring** health and safety performance;
- providing systems designed to increase safety **knowledge, awareness, and understanding**, and to encourage people to accept **responsibilities**.

## 5.1 The health and safety policy statement

This document is the starting point for all accident prevention and health promotion.

Under Section 2(3) of Health and Safety at Work, etc. Act 1974, every employer has a duty to:

> 'prepare, and as often as appropriate, revise, a written statement of his general policy, with respect to the health and safety at work of his employees and the organization, and arrangements for the time being in force for carrying out that policy, and to bring the statement and any revision of it to the notice of his employees'.

Activity 31 · 10 mins

**S/NVQ D6**

Your organization's health and safety policy statement should be available for you to read. Obtain a copy of it, and make sure you understand it. When you have done so, summarize briefly below your own responsibilities under this policy.

_____

_____

_____

_____

_____

_____

_____

_____

_____

The Health and Safety Executive (HSE) says:

> 'The best health and safety policies are concerned not only with preventing injury and ill health (as required by health and safety legislation), but also with positive health promotion which gives practical expression to the belief that people are a key resource ...
>
> The ultimate goal is an organization in which accidents and ill health are eliminated, and in which work forms part of a satisfying life, contributing to physical and mental well-being, to the benefit of both the individual and the organization.'[3]

A good health and safety policy statement will reflect these high aims. It should state the organization's health and safety objectives, and commit all managers in the organization to these objectives. It should make clear:

- management's intentions;
- how the organization is structured to implement the health and safety policy;
- the safety rules, procedures and other arrangements;
- the individual responsibilities of each level of management;
- the role of health and safety specialists, such as safety officers, advisors, company doctors and so on.

So your health and safety responsibilities, and those of your colleagues, should be clearly identifiable in your organization's policy statement.

# 6 The team leader's role

How does the local team leader fit into this picture?

---

[3] Taken from *Successful Health and Safety Management*, Health and Safety Executive, Crown copyright, 1991.

# Activity 32

Now that you have read and understood your organization's health and safety policy statement, how do you think you, as a team leader, can contribute in practical ways to your organization's safety policy?

_____

_____

_____

_____

_____

_____

There are no doubt a number of ways of contributing, including perhaps:

- **working with your manager** to agree and maintain standards of safety in your work area;
- **communicating with your team** about safety, explaining the rules, answering questions and establishing that your team members know what is expected of them;
- **developing a good team spirit**, so that efforts to maintain and improve safety standards are made in unison;
- **using all the resources** you have in a safe, as well as an efficient, manner;
- **getting individuals** in your team **to accept responsibility** for their own safety and for that of others;
- encouraging your team to **report all incidents**, including near misses;
- **channelling** data about all such incidents to your manager and other people, such as members of the safety committee and safety advisors when appropriate.

In summary, this means getting the team to **work together to prevent accidents** and to **share responsibility for safety.**

We will return to this theme, later in the workbook.

# Self-assessment 3

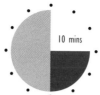

10 mins

1 Match each term on the left with the correct definition, chosen from the list on the right.

Hazard          Any undesired circumstances which give rise to ill health or injury; damage to property, plant, products or the environment; production losses or increased liabilities.

Danger          The potential to cause harm, including ill health and injury; damage to property, plant, products or the environment; production losses or increased liabilities.

Accident        The likelihood that a specified undesired event will occur due to the realization of a hazard by, or during, work activities; or by the products and services created by work activities.

Safety          An unacceptable level of risk.

Risk            The result of the activities we carry out to keep something or somebody from harm.

2 Complete the following three statements, by selecting the **most correct** ending from the list on the right.

a The seven 'classic' accident types
    i cover all the known accidents at work.
    ii could all be blamed on inadequate training.
    iii keep on happening to different people, in different places.
    iv are mostly the result of foolish people doing foolish things.

b Accidents at work are largely caused by
    i ignorance.
    ii safety systems out of control.
    iii technical factors.
    iv people doing what they're told to do, without thinking about the consequences.

c An organization's health and safety policy statement
    i is the starting point for all accident prevention and health promotion.
    ii consists of a list of safety rules.
    iii is confined to higher management.
    iv is a technical document required by the law, but which few people read.

Answers to these questions can be found on pages 178–9.

# 7 Summary

- An **accident** is any undesired circumstances which give rise to ill health or injury; damage to property, plant, products or the environment; production losses or increased liabilities.

- A **hazard** is the potential to cause harm, including ill health and injury; damage to property, plant, products or the environment; production losses or increased liabilities.

- **Risk** is the likelihood that a specified undesired event will occur due to the realization of a hazard by, or during, work activities; or by the products and services created by work activities.

- **Danger** is an unacceptable level of risk.

- **Safety** is the result of the activities we carry out to keep something or somebody from harm.

- The vast majority of accidents at work are **preventable**.

- Accidents at work are largely caused by **safety systems out of control**.

- Safety at work can only be achieved if there are **well-organized systems of safety**.

- There is often **more than one** person or group at fault in any accident.

- Accidents nearly always have **more than one cause**.

- The **health and safety policy statement** is the starting point for all accident prevention and health promotion.

- The team leader can contribute to the organization's health and safety policy by getting the team to work together to prevent accidents and to **share responsibility for safety**.

- The team leader should use all the communication channels available to ensure that 'higher management' is made aware of what **really** happens in practice, especially where it differs from what the policies and procedures say **should** happen.

# Session D
# The management of safety

## 1 Introduction

It is worth repeating the HSE statement we read earlier:

> '**The majority of accidents** and incidents are not caused by 'careless workers', but by **failures in control** (either within the organization or within a particular job), which are **the responsibility of management**.'[1]

Managers are responsible for creating health and safety policies, and for managing and supervising people to implement safe systems of work.

This session is devoted to a number of aspects of management related to safety, including: strategies, the law, risk assessment, and health and safety committees.

We begin with a subject very close to any manager's heart: costs.

[1] Taken from *Successful Health and Safety Management*, Health and Safety Executive, Crown copyright, 1991, revised 1999.

# 2 The cost of accidents

EXTENSION 10
The HSE booklet *The Costs of Accidents at Work* describes five case studies analysing the cost of accidents for each. It is worth getting hold of a copy if you are concerned about costs.

The cost of accidents and health problems at work can be measured in financial terms, both to the employer and to the injured or sick person.

Let's look at the employer's position first.

## Activity 33

3 mins

Spend a few minutes writing a list of the ways in which an accident at work may cause an employer to lose money. Try to think of **three.**

_____

_____

_____

_____

_____

_____

Money may be lost by the employer through:

■ not having the services of the injured person while he or she is unable to work, including perhaps the cost of hiring temporary staff;

■ the disruption to the work of other people;

■ the time spent by the supervisor in training replacement staff and perhaps taking part in an accident inquiry;

■ possible damage to equipment;

■ cost of employee welfare benefits;

■ possible claims for compensation;

■ lost sales and customers due to plant closures, fire damage.

Financial losses can be separated into insured and uninsured costs.

The following diagram shows one example of the hidden costs of accidents – the accident iceberg – found during an HSE study of a creamery owned by a large multinational company.

This diagram has been redrawn from the HSE booklet *The Cost of Accidents at Work*.

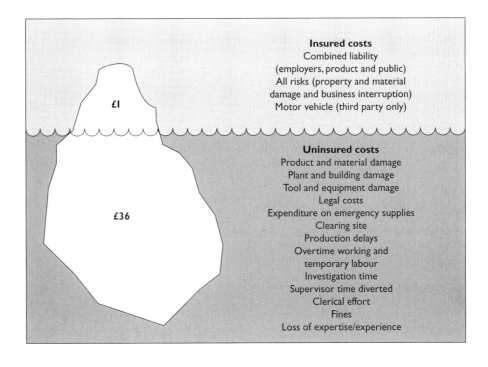

**Insured costs**
Combined liability
(employers, product and public)
All risks (property and material
damage and business interruption)
Motor vehicle (third party only)

£1

**Uninsured costs**
Product and material damage
Plant and building damage
Tool and equipment damage
Legal costs
Expenditure on emergency supplies
Clearing site
Production delays
Overtime working and
temporary labour
Investigation time
Supervisor time diverted
Clerical effort
Fines
Loss of expertise/experience

£36

Of course, the extent of insured losses, for any particular organization, depends upon the kinds of insurance policy held. The ratio of 1:36 does not seem to be untypical, however.

How about the employee's financial position?

Activity 34

3 mins

Note how an employee may lose money as a consequence of having had an accident at work.

_____

_____

_____

_____

Here are a few suggestions.

- Even with sickness benefit, the person's income may go down, especially if the injury results in a long period of absence from work.
- In the worst case, he or she may not be able to return to work at all.
- There may be other costs – travel to and from a medical centre, costs of prescriptions and so on.

Cumulatively, accidents and health problems have an effect on the national economy. The worse the health and safety record of work organizations, the worse off we all are.

The costs in human terms – the physical and mental distress of the people involved and their families – are much more difficult to evaluate, although just as real. If you've known someone who has been badly hurt at work, you'll appreciate how high the human costs can be.

# 3 Management strategies for safety

As Jeremy Stranks (1994) suggests in his book *Management Systems for Safety*, an organization can adopt one of a number of approaches to safety. It can:

- do just enough to keep within the law;
- consider safety in purely financial terms, balancing the costs of accidents against the costs of implementing safety policies;
- decide that its employees are valuable assets, and therefore worth protecting;
- take what is sometimes called a 'human factors' approach to safety.

Let's look at what we mean by the last of these.

## 3.1 The human factors approach

To develop the human factors approach, the organization must put in place a strategy based upon:

- a positive safety culture, in which health and safety is recognized as being crucial to the realization of the organization's aims;

- systems that take account of employees' varying capabilities, while acknowledging that nobody is infallible;
- a commitment to high standards through all levels of management, starting at the top.

Safety strategies need to be **proactive**, rather than reactive: that is, they should control the situation by taking the initiative, rather than simply reacting to what happens. Both workplaces and people need to be made safe.

## 3.2 Making workplaces safe

To carry out work, organizations typically use premises, equipment, processes and materials. So, under the law:

- **premises** must be safe

  Buildings must be stable and sound, and must offer employees protection;

- **equipment** must be safe

  It should be appropriate to its task, and properly maintained;

- **processes** must be safe

  Every aspect of a work process has to be considered in terms of its hazards and risks;

- **materials** must be safe

  The hazards from substances need to be recognized, and the risks contained.

Most importantly, **safe systems of work** must be employed integrating all of the above. A safe system of work can be defined as:

**the integration of people, machinery and materials in a correct working environment to provide the safest possible working conditions.**

## 3.3 Making people safe

Things can still go wrong, even in an apparently safe workplace because people are unpredictable, vulnerable and may be ignorant of the dangers.

# Activity 35

2 mins

So far, we have listed safe premises; equipment, processes, and materials. What else is needed in a workplace to help keep people safe? [Hint: think about your own job as first line manager.]

_____

_____

> In all matters of safety, it's important to take into account the capabilities and needs of individuals. It can be a serious mistake to assume that everyone will behave in the same way in response to hazards and risks.

An important ingredient for workplace safety is **adequate supervision**. People need different amounts of supervision, according to their age, experience and status. Certain groups are more vulnerable, particularly:

■ the young;

■ people with disabilities;

■ workers exposed to special risks.

With regard to the last of these, **personal protective equipment (PPE)** often has a significant role to play. We will look at the various types of PPE in the next session.

In many workplaces, adequate **washing facilities** must be provided, especially where:

■ there is a risk of hazardous chemicals coming into contact with the skin;

■ food is handled.

## 3.4 Training

A key aspect of accident prevention is induction and continuing job training. At an absolute minimum, people need training in:

■ understanding health and safety law;

■ using personal protective equipment;

■ specific hazards in their workplace, and how to deal with them;

■ dealing with emergencies and abnormal occurrences;

■ safe and correct operation of machinery;

■ manual handling techniques (if applicable).

Training should (by law):

■ be repeated periodically where appropriate;

■ be adapted to take account of new or changed risks;

■ take place during working hours.

# Activity 36

**S/NVQ
E6**

This Activity may provide the basis of appropriate evidence for your S/NVQ portfolio. If you are intending to take this course of action, it might be better to write your answers on separate sheets of paper.

What training have you arranged for your team in health and safety, in the past year?

_____

_____

_____

_____

_____

_____

Explain how you ensure that the training your team receives is appropriate and sufficient for them to work in a healthy, safe and productive way.

_____

_____

_____

_____

_____

What health and safety training are you planning for the coming months?

_____

_____

_____

_____

_____

# 4 Accident prevention and the law

At the very least, organizations must comply with the law on health and safety. The penalties and costs of not doing so can be very high, including fines and imprisonment.

As we have seen, health and safety legislation is embodied in:

■ case law or common law

Every court is bound by the decisions previously made in higher courts, or courts at the same level. Thus a judgement made in a particular case can affect the outcome of all subsequent cases of the same kind.

■ statute law

Statute law comprises **Acts of Parliament**, such as the Health and Safety at Work, etc. Act 1974 (HSWA). 'Enabling Acts' like HSWA give rise to 'statutory instruments', in the form of **Regulations,** such as the Management of Health and Safety at Work Regulations 1999 (MHSWR).

■ European Union directives

**Directives** are the instruments of EU legislation, which are binding on all member states. Normally, directives are complied within the UK by embodying them in Acts of Parliament.

# 5 Risk assessment

MHSWR, and four of the other 'six-pack' Regulations, require organizations to assess the risks attached to work operations.

According to MHSWR, an employer must assess:

■ 'the risks to the health and safety of his employees to which they are exposed at work';
■ 'the risks to the health and safety of persons not in his employment arising out of or in connection with the conduct of him and his undertaking'.

A definition of risk assessment is:

> 'an identification of the hazards present in an undertaking and an estimate of the extent of the risks involved, taking into account whatever precautions are already being taken'. (Jeremy Stranks (1994), *Management Systems for Safety.*)

The process is one of:

- identifying the hazard;
- measuring and evaluating the risk from this hazard;
- putting measures into place that will either eliminate the hazard, or control it.

The risk assessment has to be systematic, so that no risks are overlooked. Organizations may approach the task in various ways. They could, for example, examine:

MHSWR states: 'A suitable and sufficient risk assessment should identify the significant risks arising out of work. Trivial risks can be ignored as can risks arising from routine activities associated with life in general unless the work activity compounds these risks ...'

- every activity that might result in injury;
- every type of substance used;
- every type of machine used;
- every location on which work takes place.

Each of these approaches is valid, provided that it is carried out systematically, and covers all possible risks.

## 5.1 Calculating the risk

The assessment of risk is not an exact science, because it involves making judgements about:

- the likelihood or probability that an accident might occur;
- how serious the outcome might be, if it did occur;
- how often the risk is present.

We will briefly discuss two methods for calculating risk.

> **You are not advised to apply these methods to your work situation without further training.**

One method is to simply rate, first the hazard severity and second, the likelihood of its occurrence.

Hazards – the potential to cause harm will vary in severity. The effect of a hazard may, for example, be rated as:

3 – major: resulting, for example, in death or major injury;

2 – serious: causing people to be off work for more than three days;

1 – slight: all other minor injuries.

This is the first method of calculating risk that we discuss.

Harm may not arise from exposure to a hazard in every case, and in practice the likelihood of harm will be affected by the organization of the work, how effectively the hazard is controlled, and the extent and nature of exposure to it.

The likelihood of harm may be rated as:

3 – high: where it is certain or near certain that harm will occur;

2 – medium: where harm will occur frequently;

1 – low: where harm will seldom occur.

The risk can then be defined as the combination of the severity of the hazard with the likelihood of its occurrence, so that:

> RISK = HAZARD SEVERITY × LIKELIHOOD OF OCCURRENCE

The single figure result (ranging from 1 to 9) provides a method of comparing the risk associated with various work operations.

> **Example**
>
> The risk to health from the spillage of a hazardous chemical in a company works is calculated as follows:
>
> hazard severity – major (rating 3)
>
> likelihood of occurrence – low (rating 1)
>
> Risk = Hazard Severity × Likelihood of Occurrence = 3 × 1 = 3

This simple method may not suit all organizations, and other methods have been devised.

A second method combines the three factors of:

This is the second method of calculating risk that we discuss.

- likelihood (probability) of occurrence;
- severity; and
- frequency.

A scale from 1 to 10 is assigned for each one, and the three scores are multiplied together to get a rating out of 1,000.

The formula is:

Risk rating = Probability (P) × Severity (S) × Frequency (F)

The following tables are used.

**Probability scale**

| Probability index | Descriptive phrase |
|---|---|
| 10 | Inevitable |
| 9 | Almost certain |
| 8 | Very likely |
| 7 | Probable |
| 6 | More than an even chance |
| 5 | Even chance |
| 4 | Less than an even chance |
| 3 | Improbable |
| 2 | Very improbable |
| 1 | Almost impossible |

**Severity scale**

| Severity index | Descriptive phrase |
|---|---|
| 10 | Death |
| 9 | Permanent total incapacity |
| 8 | Permanent severe incapacity |
| 7 | Permanent slight incapacity |
| 6 | Absent from work for more than 3 weeks with subsequent recurring incapacity |
| 5 | Absent from work for more than 3 weeks but with subsequent complete recovery |
| 4 | Absent from work for more than 3 days with subsequent complete recovery |
| 3 | Absent from work for less than 3 days with complete recovery |
| 2 | Minor injury with no lost time and complete recovery |
| 1 | No human injury expected |

**Frequency scale**

| Frequency index | Descriptive phrase |
|---|---|
| 10 | Hazard permanently present |
| 9 | Hazard arises every 30 seconds |
| 8 | Hazard arises every minute |
| 7 | Hazard arises every 30 minutes |
| 6 | Hazard arises every hour |
| 5 | Hazard arises every shift |
| 4 | Hazard arises once a week |
| 3 | Hazard arises once a month |
| 2 | Hazard arises every year |
| 1 | Hazard arises every 5 years |

### Example

Suppose a certain work operation involved a hazard which:

- would probably cause an accident;
- would result in an absence from work for more than three weeks, with subsequent recovery;
- arose once an hour.

By looking up the tables, we would find that P = 7, S = 5 and F = 6. Applying our formula, we would get:

$$\text{Risk rating} = \text{Probability (P)} \times \text{Severity (S)} \times \text{Frequency (F)}.$$
$$= 7 \times 5 \times 6 = 210$$

Next, we apply the risk rating to a table showing the priority of action:

### Priority of action scale

| 801–1,000 | Immediate action |
|-----------|------------------|
| 601–800   | Action within 7 days |
| 401–600   | Action within next month |
| 201–400   | Action within next year |
| Below 200 | No immediate action necessary, but keep under review. |

For our example, the priority would be 'action within the next year'.

# Activity 37

3 mins

Assume that you found the following situation during a risk assessment. You determined that there was more than an even chance of an accident occurring, that there would be permanent slight incapacity if it did occur, and that the hazard arises every 30 minutes. What is the risk rating, and how quickly would action need to be taken?

Compare your answer with the following.

Risk rating = Probability (P) × Severity (S) × Frequency (F).

= 6 × 7 × 7 = 294

According to the priority of action scale, action would need to be taken within a year.

The methods described above have their drawbacks, and need to be administered with care. If your organization uses procedures for risk calculation, you may be able to get training in their application.

Sensible business managers will always apply a final 'common sense' judgement to the arithmetical answers from risk management calculations. By doing so, they can give increased weighting to the 'frequently occurring minor risk' (which can be bad for morale) on the one hand and the 'improbable risk with severe consequences' on the other, which could have catastrophic consequences for people and other ramifications.

## 5.2 Taking action

Risk assessment is an important management activity, whether or not it is quantified on a scale. When hazards are present, action must be taken to assess the risk and eliminate or reduce it.

Activity 38

S/NVQ E6

This Activity may provide the basis of appropriate evidence for your S/NVQ portfolio. If you are intending to take this course of action, it might be better to write your answers on separate sheets of paper.

As part of your job, you are expected to ensure that the work conditions under your control conform to organizational and legal requirements. In fulfilling this duty, you may have to take part in risk assessments. You should, at the least, be aware of hazards present in your work area, so that you can pass information about them to your team.

Give **three** examples of identified hazards that you are aware of in your work.

_____

_____

_____

_____

_____

_____

_____

_____

_____

What are the risks associated with these hazards, according to the last risk assessment?

_____

_____

_____

_____

_____

_____

_____

_____

_____

Describe any further actions you plan to take, and when, in order to eliminate or reduce the risk from these hazards.

_____

_____

_____

_____

_____

_____

_____

_____

Ideally, risks should be eliminated completely. You might ban the use of a particular harmful substance, for example. Or you could try to find a different, less hazardous, method of doing the work.

If **elimination of the risk** is not practicable, other measures you might take, in order of preference, are to:

1  **enclose the risk**, say by placing a guard around a machine, or putting a hazardous chemical in a suitable container, to prevent anyone coming in contact with it;

2  **install a safety device**, such as an interlock that precludes access to a device unless the power is off;

3  implement a safe system of work, so that the **risk is reduced to an acceptable level**.

If there is still a risk present, you may need to take other measures.

4  You could **provide specific written safety instructions** for your team, and make sure they understand what the risks are, and that they know how to protect themselves against the risks.

> If you have team members whose first language is not English, it may be wise to provide translations of safety instructions, whether or not they request this.

5  As we have already discussed, **safety supervision** must be adequate for the people you are responsible for. Also, even if you believe that your written instructions are clear, a face-to-face discussion can help to clear up any misunderstandings. Not everyone is a careful reader.

6  Everyone at work needs health and safety **training.** Training may be in respect of particular hazards, or may cover a number of areas.

7  **Information** should be provided, where hazards are known to exist, in the form of posters, safety signs, warning notices and so on.

8  As a last line of defence, your team may need to have **personal protective equipment** such as goggles, helmets, aprons and so forth.

# 6 People with a special role to play

Everyone at work has a part to play in health and safety.

But these subjects are too important to be left to compete for priority with all the other activities going on in a busy organization.

It's also valuable to have people who, as part of their job, deliberately and consciously set out to promote health and safety and to look into potential hazards.

# 6.1 The safety officer

Full- or part-time **safety officers** (also sometimes called safety practitioners, safety specialists, safety advisors or safety engineers) may be appointed.

A safety officer is part of the management team, directing employees in safety activities and sharing the responsibility with the other managers and supervisors. This may not necessarily be a full-time task. The job may be delegated to a number of people, each having an assistant's role for a specialized activity.

Because the officer is specially trained and/or qualified in safety matters, he or she will be in a position to advise others.

The safety officer co-ordinates and promotes the work of accident prevention by:

EXTENSION 11
If you are interested in studying the subject of safety representatives or safety committees in more depth, the Approved Code of Practice, *Safety Representatives and Safety Committees*, by the Health and Safety Executive, gives useful information.

- periodically inspecting plant, tools and machinery to identify hazards;
- examining work operations to determine whether there are any unsafe practices;
- recommending improvements;
- taking part in safety training and education of employees and supervisors;
- acting as co-ordinator of safety work;
- leading and taking part in safety meetings.

# 6.2 The safety representative

Recognized trade unions may appoint safety representatives to represent employees on matters of health and safety at work.

A safety representative is not necessarily a safety specialist like the safety officer. Nevertheless, the representative is expected to have worked for his or her present employer for at least the preceding two years, or have had two years' experience in a similar job.

# Activity 39

3 mins

Although the representative is not expected to be a safety specialist, he or she is in a good position to contribute certain kinds of knowledge when it comes to accident prevention.

What knowledge might an experienced employee, interested in safety, be able to contribute?

_____

_____

_____

_____

Such a person may have knowledge of:

- the hazards in that type of work;
- the specific hazards in that workplace;
- what has been tried in the past, successfully or unsuccessfully, to eliminate hazards in that workplace;
- accidents that have happened in the past;
- the health and safety policy of the employer, and the arrangements for carrying out the safety policy.

Safety representatives are of course expected to keep such knowledge up-to-date. They are also expected to keep themselves informed of the legal requirements related to health and safety – particularly those of the groups of people they represent.

The employer must give safety representatives time off with pay for training in safety matters.

# Activity 40

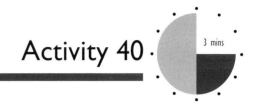

3 mins

We have established that a safety representative is experienced, interested in safety, receives training and represents employees in health and safety matters.

With this in mind, what specific functions should the representative carry out, do you think? You should try for **two** or **three**.

_____

_____

_____

_____

_____

<table>
<tr><td>The relevant legislation is The Safety Representatives and Safety Committees Regulations 1977.</td></tr>
</table>

The following are the main functions of the safety representative in law. They are probably what you would expect. The law (Safety Representatives and Safety Committees Regulations 1977) says that the representative shall:

- 'investigate potential hazards and dangerous occurrences at the workplace – whether or not they are drawn to his attention by the employees he represents – and examine the causes of accidents at the workplace';
- 'investigate complaints by any employee he represents, related to that employee's health, safety or welfare at work';
- 'make representations to the employer on specific or general matters of health, safety and welfare';
- 'carry out inspections';
- 'attend meetings of safety committees'.

The employer must let the representative have time to carry out this work, without loss of pay.

Of course, in practice, people like yourself, who have direct responsibility for the safety of staff, will normally work closely with safety representatives when it comes to inspections and investigations.

**Full co-operation is essential in health and safety matters.**

## 6.3 Safety committees

In law, an employer must set up a safety committee if requested to do so by two or more safety representatives. In practice, safety committees are established quite frequently by employers even without such a request.

To be most effective, safety committees should be established for each place of work, rather than having one committee trying to serve a large organization with lots of sites.

The work of a safety committee might include:

- studying statistics and trends;
- considering reports by safety representatives;
- helping to develop safety rules and safe systems of work;
- monitoring the effectiveness of safety training;
- monitoring the effectiveness of communication and publicity on health and safety;
- making recommendations to management to improve health and safety at work in both a specific and general way.

Activity 41

Which group or groups do you think should be represented on a safety committee?

Employees? ❐

Supervisors/managers? ❐

Senior management? ❐

A safety committee should have people representing employees and managers at all levels.

If there is a safety officer, he or she should take part. Any medical staff appointed by the organization would also have a role to play. Technical specialists may be brought in when specific subjects are being discussed.

Constructively used, a safety committee which meets regularly – preferably every month – is the best forum through which any organization can improve it's 'safety culture'.

# Self-assessment 4

10 mins

1 Which **two** of the following statements are correct?

a Uninsured costs are typically much lower than insured costs. ❐

b Proactive safety strategies, rather than reactive ones, are best. ❐

c It is worth remembering that nearly everyone will react to a particular hazard in the same way. ❐

d Safe processes, safe premises, and safe materials, are all necessary and important in making workplaces safe. ❐

2 Complete the following sentences with suitable words, chosen from the list below.

a A safe _____ of work is the _____ of people, machinery and materials in a correct working _____ to provide the safest possible working _____.

b Under HSWA, _____ must have regard for the safety of _____ who may be affected by the activities of their companies.

c All _____ have duties: to take _____ care for their own safety and that of others; to _____ with their employers in matters of safety; not to _____ with or misuse anything provided for safety.

d Every _____ must make an _____ of the health and safety _____ of work activities to _____ and anyone else who may be affected, and record the findings.

e MHSWR requires employers to appoint _____ people.

| | | |
|---|---|---|
| ASSESSMENT | CO-OPERATE | COMPETENT |
| CONDITIONS | EMPLOYEES | EMPLOYEES |
| EMPLOYER | EMPLOYERS | ENVIRONMENT |
| INTEGRATION | INTERFERE | NON-EMPLOYEES |
| REASONABLE | RISKS | SYSTEM |

3 Explain, briefly, the purpose of assigning risk ratings to hazards.

_____

_____

_____

_____

4   Place the following actions in order of preference, as responses to a known risk from a hazard, by putting a number in each box. (The most preferable action should be assigned number 1.)

| | |
|---|---|
| Implement a system of work that reduces the risk. | ❐ |
| Install a safety device. | ❐ |
| Eliminate the risk. | ❐ |
| Provide specific written safety instructions. | ❐ |
| Enclose the risk. | ❐ |
| Provide training. | ❐ |
| Provide general information about safety. | ❐ |
| Provide personal protective equipment. | ❐ |
| Supervise those at risk from the hazard. | ❐ |

The answers to these questions can be found on page 179.

# 7 Summary

- In terms of financial cost, **employers** and **employees both suffer** when accidents occur. Frequently, employers' costs are far greater than those against which they are insured.

- Safety strategies need to be **proactive**, rather than reactive: that is, they should control the situation by taking the initiative, rather than simply reacting to what happens.

- For a workplace to be safe, **premises, equipment, processes** and **materials** must all be made safe.

- A key aspect of accident prevention is **training**.

- The **Health and Safety at Work, etc. Act 1974 (HSWA)** places obligations on both employers and employees, and covers the safety of virtually everyone at work. Employers must safeguard the health, safety, and welfare of their employees, and of non-employees affected by work activities.

- HSWA says that all employees have **duties**:

  - to take reasonable care for their own safety and that of others;
  - to co-operate with their employers in matters of safety;
  - not to interfere with or misuse anything provided for safety.

- The **Management of Health and Safety at Work Regulations 1999** (MHSWR) requires employers to:

  - assess the risks of the job;
  - provide health surveillance if necessary.
  - appoint competent people;
  - provide employees with information and training about health and safety matters;
  - set up emergency procedures.

- **Risk assessment** is 'an identification of the hazards present in an undertaking and an estimate of the extent of the risks involved, taking into account whatever precautions are already being taken'. Two methods for obtaining a numerical value for risk rating were discussed.

- To **control risks and hazards**, the following actions may be taken, in order of preference:

  1 eliminate the risk;
  2 enclose the risk;
  3 install a safety device;
  4 implement a system of work that reduces the risk;
  5 provide specific written safety instructions;
  6 supervise those at risk from the hazard;
  7 provide training;
  8 provide general information about safety;
  9 provide personal protective equipment.

- People with a special role to play in health and safety include **safety officers, safety representatives** and **safety committees**.

# Session E
# Practical accident prevention

## ▪ 1 Introduction

EXTENSION 12
The HSE book
*Essentials of Health and Safety at Work* identifies many types of hazard, and the precautions that may be used to protect against them.

We began by looking at some accounts of actual accidents, and tried to establish ways of preventing them. So far, we have talked mainly in terms of **management systems**. This is right and proper, for accidents are usually the result of systems out of control.

But there is plenty to be learned by examining the reasons behind particular accidents and accident types. That's what accident investigators do: they want to know 'how did this accident happen, and how can we stop it happening again?' (We'll look at the job of the accident investigator in Session F.) It is useful to operate from the assumption that what **can** go wrong **will** go wrong.

So, in this session, we'll put accidents into groups, and see what can be done by way of preventative action. The groups are:

- accidents involving work equipment;
- electrical hazards;
- falling accidents, including accidents with ladders;
- manual handling accidents;
- maintenance accidents;
- fire hazards.

We also look at personal protective equipment and, finally, at housekeeping.

# 2 Equipment safety

These days, it's hard to think of a job that doesn't involve equipment of some kind.

The PUWER regulations define 'work equipment' so widely as to include everything from a hammer to a vehicle hoist and from a computer to a blast furnace.

We normally associate equipment safety with heavy industry or agriculture. But equipment is found in offices, shops, studios, playschools, hospitals – in fact in almost every work area.

You may not have had to deal with an accident involving equipment – yet. That doesn't mean to say that all the equipment under your responsibility is completely safe, or that everyone who uses it is capable of using it safely under all conditions.

## Activity 42

5 mins

Think about the equipment in your own place of work. What do you do to try to make sure that people don't have accidents when they use it?

_____

_____

_____

What more could you do?

_____

_____

_____

Here are some general guidelines that apply in all situations.

■ The first important thing is to do what you just did – think about how to prevent injury. Think what could occur if things were to go wrong. Learn to recognize when parts of any piece of equipment are hazardous.

**It's useful to think about what might go wrong.**

As we discussed in Session A, a very common type of equipment accident is entanglement. Any equipment with rotating parts is potentially dangerous, whether or not those parts are projecting or normally accessible.

■ Don't rely on training, and on everyone being sensible. Many accidents arise because people behave in a foolish or careless manner.

**Accident prevention shouldn't depend on people always obeying the rules.**

■ Don't allow guards to be removed. Guards are there to protect people. If guards need to be removed often, they should be interlocked, so that the machine can never be turned on accidentally when the guard is absent. If the guards are inconvenient to use, or are easily defeated, try to get them improved if you can.

**Keeping the guards in place is not just good practice – it's the law.**

■ Ensure that regular inspection and maintenance is carried out by competent and trained staff.

**Inspection and maintenance of equipment are essential.**

■ But remember that maintenance staff get hurt, too. It's important to give them all the information you can before they start work.

■ Allow only trained and authorized staff to use the equipment.

**Keep untrained and unauthorized people away.**

■ Keep hazardous equipment well away from the public, and from visitors.

**Organizations have a duty to protect non-employees.**

■ Make sure that control switches are marked so that there's no chance of switching on the wrong equipment. If there's a need for an emergency shut-off button, make sure it's clearly labelled, within easy reach, and is coloured red.

**Switches should be well marked and easily accessible.**

■ New equipment, hired equipment, any equipment being brought back into service after maintenance, and equipment standing idle for long periods of time, must be carefully checked before it's used.

**Machines which haven't been in use must be checked.**

# Activity 43

4 mins

Try to draw up a brief safety checklist of about **three** or **four** points for operators to carry out whenever they go to use equipment. If possible, think in terms of equipment used at your own place of work.

_____

_____

_____

_____

_____

_____

A good checklist for an operator might include the following:

■ make sure all guards are in place;
■ make sure all interlocks are working properly – if necessary, by testing them;
■ learn how to **switch off** the equipment **before** switching it on;
■ put on any specified protective clothing;
■ do not wear anything which could possibly get caught up in the equipment – loose clothing, chains or rings for instance; long hair should be covered by a hairnet or hat;
■ make sure there's nothing that can get in the way of moving parts, such as loose materials;
■ do not use the equipment without being trained and authorized;
■ make sure there is no sign on the equipment that says it is defective or dangerous to use (the supervisor should be told at once if the equipment appears not to be working correctly);
■ make sure work surfaces and the general area is clean and tidy, and help to keep it that way.

# 2.1 Prescribed dangerous machines

Some machines used in offices, agriculture and industry have special rules. There are certain machines which are 'prescribed dangerous machines', including:

- guillotines;
- mixers;
- portable machinery;
- bacon slicers;
- power-operated wrappers and slicers.

Under the Factories Act, 1961, young people (that is, those 16 or over, and under 18 years) are prohibited from working at any prescribed dangerous machine, unless they have:

- been fully instructed as to the dangers arising in connection with it and the precautions to be observed;
- have received sufficient training in work at the machine;
- are under adequate supervision by a person who has a thorough knowledge and experience of the machine.

**Ensure that young persons are trained and supervised.**

Of course, all people using such machines should be trained. Young people need special protection because they are the ones most at risk.

Other kinds of machines are covered by Regulations which require certain kinds of guards, to prevent people coming in contact with moving parts. These include:

- abrasive wheels;
- woodworking machines;
- horizontal milling machines;
- power take-off shafts.

**Using untrained operators, or unguarded machines, may be against the law.**

# 3 Preventing falls

It is possible to place falls from accidents into one of three categories:

- people tripping or falling at the same height or level;
- people falling from one height to another;
- something falling onto someone.

## 3.1 Falls at the same height

We tend to think of falls as being something dramatic, involving falling from a height, but falling at the same level can result in serious injury.

# Activity 44

3 mins

Jot down at least **two** typical causes of people having accidents by tripping or slipping at the same level. For example, one cause might be a damaged floor or ground surface.

_____

_____

_____

_____

_____

You may have noted some of the following causes:

- a damaged floor or ground surface, such as an uneven pavement;
- a wet, greasy or icy surface;
- an unevenness in the surface, such as an unexpected step;
- poor lighting;
- some object on the surface;
- unsuitable or worn footwear.

These are all causes relating to the conditions on the floor or ground. You may have also considered possible causes arising from the state or actions of the person who falls, such as fatigue, being drunk, having poor eyesight or running instead of walking.

# Activity 45

4 mins

Draw up a checklist to prevent accidents resulting from falling at the same level, based on the list above. One point might be: 'Check surfaces, to ensure they're in good repair.' Try to include at least **five** points in your list.

_____

_____

_____

_____

_____

_____

_____

_____

A possible checklist is given below. Compare it with yours.

- Don't allow people to walk on a wet floor unless they have suitable footwear.
- Check surfaces, to ensure they're in good repair.
- Put up barriers or portable signs to prevent people walking on temporarily wet and slippery floors.
- Put down salt in icy weather, on outdoor walking surfaces.
- Try to eliminate surface unevenness; if this isn't possible, use signs such as 'Mind the step!'
- Keep areas where people walk well lit.
- Keep surfaces free from clutter.
- Don't allow running or 'larking about'.
- Permit no intoxication, under any circumstances.

## 3.2 Falls from one level to another

Falls of this kind may be:

- through or into openings: holes, trap-doors and so on;
- through or from roofs;
- from ladders or down stairs;
- while working at heights, such as on a scaffold.

# Activity 46

3 mins

What do you think are the main reasons that might cause someone to fall into or through an opening such as a hole, pit, trench or trap-door?

_____

_____

_____

_____

_____

_____

_____

You could say there were two main reasons:

- an opening not being properly guarded or covered;
- the person being unaware of the opening.

Often, both these reasons apply.

Typically, accidents occur when:

- someone leaves an opening unmarked and unguarded, such as removing a man-hole cover and then leaving it as a hazard for the unwary;
- a cover is inadequate: for example, a trap-door not being capable of supporting a person's weight;
- it is not clear that a board or sheet of metal is covering a hole.

The way to prevent such accidents is to ensure that:

- openings are guarded, well marked and well lit;
- covers can withstand any expected load or impact;
- covers are clearly identified.

## 3.3 Ladder safety

A fall from a ladder may occur when:

- the ladder isn't secured: ladders should preferably be secured by tying at the top, or else at the sides or bottom;
- someone works too high on the ladder without a handhold;
- the ladder is weak or damaged;
- the ladder is at an unstable angle: ladders should have a slope of four units up to one out from the base;
- the ladder is placed against a fragile surface, such as a plastic gutter;
- the ladder is placed on an insecure footing, such as loose flagstones or soft earth;
- the person climbing the ladder is carrying or holding something, having no hands free for holding on to the ladder;
- the ladder is the wrong one for the job – when it is too long or too short, for example.

Another possible hazard is leaving a ladder where a person or a vehicle could collide with it.

Ladders are involved in so many serious and fatal accidents that the first question to ask is: 'Can this job be done **without** using a ladder?' If it can, then their hazards are eliminated.

## 3.4 Working on roofs

Every year, many people die at work by falling through or off roofs.

If it is part of the job of your team to work on roofs, you should have received instruction on the dangers and safeguards.

Generally, accidents are caused when people:

- fall through roofs by walking on fragile materials, wrongly assuming the material will hold their weight;
- fall off roofs by not using suitable crawling boards or proper edge protection;
- injure themselves in other ways, when they ignore hazards such as high winds, or fumes from flue outlets.

To prevent these kinds of accidents, roof workers should:

- never make assumptions about the strength of materials;
- always use proper equipment;
- never ignore hazards.

Isolation barriers should again be used when there is a risk of objects falling on to people below, or where ladders or scaffolding might be walked or driven into.

## 3.5 Falling objects

Injuries from falling objects are unfortunately also very common. This fact is recognized in many industries such as building, chemical engineering and so on, and workers in such industries are issued with safety helmets as a matter of course.

Such accidents often come about through errors on the part of people working at high levels or controlling heavy moving equipment. Where activities are taking place above eye level, people on the ground need to be especially alert.

Falling objects can injure people in stockrooms, shops, warehouses and other places where people are **not** usually issued with 'hard hats'. Ensure that you look at your own working area for any such hazards and that your team is briefed to do likewise.

Activity 47

Draw up a checklist of **three** or **four** points that might help prevent accidents from falling objects. Consider the area where you work, if this kind of hazard exists there.

_____

_____

_____

_____

_____

_____

Compare your list with this one.

- Don't walk under loads that are suspended, such as from a crane.
- Don't throw anything down from above; get it lowered safely.
- Always wear protective clothing such as helmets and safety shoes where there is a hazard of falling objects.
- Don't leave tools near to the edge of surfaces, or in an unstable position.
- Stack materials with care, making sure, first that they can be stacked, and second, that they're stable.
- Use isolation barriers where there is a hazard of falling objects.

# 4 Electrical hazards

Electricity is hazardous. It can cause electric shock, explosion and fire.

And yet nearly everybody, at home or at work, uses electricity and electrical appliances every day of their lives.

## Activity 48

3 mins

Assuming you are not a trained electrician, what can you do to minimize the dangers from electricity? Try to jot down at least **three** actions or precautions you would take.

_____

_____

_____

_____

_____

_____

Some of the things you may have written down are the following.

- Socket outlets should not be overloaded by using adapters. This is dangerous and could cause a fire. If necessary, a multiplug socket block should be used instead – although even these can become overloaded.
- No one should be allowed to open covers which give access to live electrical parts, unless they are fully trained and competent to do so.
- Faulty apparatus – or any machine which is suspected as being faulty – should be taken out of service and a 'do not use' label placed on it.

- Everyone who uses a machine should be shown how to isolate the power from it in case of emergency. There should be a well-marked switch or isolator close to every machine.
- All electrical installations to be checked regularly by a trained electrician.
- Workteams should be trained to make sure that power sockets are switched off before plugging tools into them.

## 4.1 Dealing with electric shock

If training in dealing with electric shock is available to you and your team, it's a good idea to take it. As a first step your company should be able to get a copy of the 'electric shock placard' which tells you what to do. But resuscitating someone takes training and practice.

- **Never** touch anyone you believe may have suffered an electric shock. If you are not clear yourself what should be done, get competent help **immediately**.

## 4.2 Static electricity

The problem doesn't all come from mains electricity. You've probably noticed that you can get a slight electric shock by touching a metal object like a door handle after walking across a synthetic carpet. This is called **static electricity**. Static electricity isn't always dangerous in itself, **but**:

- the shock from static electricity can cause an involuntary movement which could result in an accident;
- sparks generated by static electricity can be very dangerous near flammable liquids, or powders like grain or tea dust; they can cause the vapour or dust to ignite, sometimes with explosive results.

For this second reason, whenever these materials are being transported or stored, earthed metal containers should be used, as plastic containers can cause a static charge to build up. Where there is a hazard from static electricity, precautions can be taken to prevent its build-up – such as earthing. Special anti-static clothing and footwear may be worn. You may need specialist advice on this.

## 4.3 Working outdoors

Some points to remember when electricity is used outdoors:

Socket outlets used outdoors may need to be of a special design and protected by a residual current circuit-breaker. If electrical tools are used outdoors, it's safest to use low voltage equipment or isolating transformers, with the long lead on the low voltage side.

As with all aspects of electricity:

**If you aren't sure – get advice about it!**

■ Working under or near overhead power lines is very dangerous. All machines should be kept at least 15 metres away, or flashover may occur, in which the high voltage strikes the machine. Before working near overhead power lines, talk to the local electricity company.

■ If you have to dig holes in the ground, you should always assume that there are buried live electricity cables. You can use cable-detecting equipment to confirm this. Again, you should talk to the electricity company, and use cable avoidance tools. Don't forget that other cables and pipelines may also be present.

## 5 Maintenance work

As we've already discussed, over a quarter of fatal accidents in industry occur during, or as a result of, maintenance. There are special problems related to maintenance work.

# Activity 49

Maintenance work is often done outside the normal working hours of a company, and also may be out of sight of the day staff. A good example of this is in a retail store, where maintenance is usually carried out screened off from the public and staff, and often when the store is closed. Make a note of **three** or **four** problems that might arise in this situation, and which may make the work of maintenance hazardous.

_____

_____

_____

_____

Some problems you may have jotted down are as follows. All of these difficulties may arise in any maintenance situation.

■ Normal safeguards may be deliberately bypassed during the maintenance work, and other safeguards not put in their place. For example, electrical wiring may be left uncovered, or handrails removed.

■ Maintenance work may have to be carried out in cramped, poorly lit and unusual conditions. Also, where space is limited, adequate supervision may be impractical.

■ Work may not always be properly completed. This might result, for example, in accidents to sales staff switching on equipment following the maintenance work.

■ Management will be trained to think about the safety of the customers in the store, but may not pay so much attention to safety of maintenance personnel. This may be especially true when the shop is closed, and there are no customers to worry about.

■ There may be insufficient communication between operating staff and maintenance workers, to indicate the condition of equipment before maintenance work is commenced.

■ Outside contractors may often be employed to carry out maintenance; these people may perform very specialized work. Management and other staff may assume that 'they must know what they're doing' and abdicate any responsibility for the safety of the contractor staff.

First line managers can play an important role in reducing the number and severity of accidents during maintenance.

# Activity 50

5 mins

In a typical situation, a manager is in charge of some plant or machinery that requires maintenance and/or repair. For this it is necessary to call in other people, from inside or outside the organization.

With the points listed above in mind, draw up a brief checklist, of **three** or **four** key points, for a manager in these circumstances.

_____

_____

_____

_____

_____

_____

Such a checklist may include the following points.

> A permit to work system is a management tool designed for high risk tasks, to ensure that a safe system is in place and is adequately implemented.

- Have you explained precisely what the condition of the plant or machinery is, as far as you are able to determine?
- Have you told the maintenance staff how to isolate the plant or machinery?
- Have you provided any appropriate safety equipment, including first aid materials, and explained how emergency help can be obtained?
- After the work is completed, have you discussed the condition of the equipment with the maintenance staff, before attempting to put it back into service?
- Is a permit to work required? For example, a permit to work is essential where excavations are carried out on industrial premises.

# 6 Manual handling

More than a third of the accidents reported each year are associated with manual handling – the transporting or supporting of loads by hand or by bodily force. Back strain, sprains and limb breakages are relatively common.

If you ask someone to lift up a heavy object and carry it across the floor, he or she may go about the task in the wrong way, and finish up hurting themselves. And yet the correct techniques are not difficult to learn.

Before any manual handling is done, you will need to stand back and think about the task, and the possible alternatives. The following flowchart shows the steps that should be taken whenever you decide to have something moved manually.

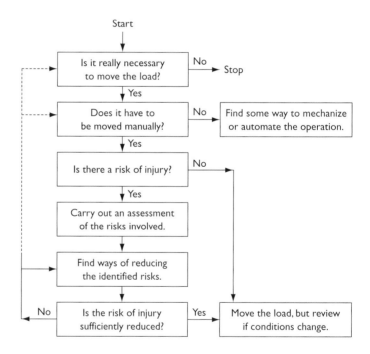

Again, you will notice, the subject of risk assessment has arisen. We'll look at this again shortly.

# 6.1 Handling techniques

Once you are sure that manual handling is necessary, proper techniques must be applied. These need to be learned, and training should be given.

The following is an example of good handling technique for picking up a box and carrying it to a table or bench.

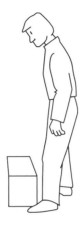

**First, stop and think about how you will tackle the job**. You need to plan the lift, and ask yourself:

- where you intend to place the load;
- whether you should get someone to help you;
- if you have access to handling aids (such as trolleys) that would be useful;
- whether there are any obstructions (such as packing materials) that should be moved first;
- whether there is a table or bench that you could use to rest the load on, say mid-way between floor and shoulder height.

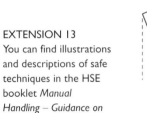

**Use your feet as a balanced and stable base for lifting**. Make sure your footwear is appropriate, and that your clothes do not impede your movement. Stand feet well apart, with your leading leg slightly forward.

EXTENSION 13
You can find illustrations and descriptions of safe techniques in the HSE booklet *Manual Handling – Guidance on Regulations*, which also gives useful guidance on the law. The ones here have been adapted from this booklet.

**Take up a good posture**. Bend your knees but do not overflex them. Keep your back straight, with your chin tucked in. You may need to lean forward a little over the load to get a good grip. Your shoulders should be level and should face in the same direction as your hips.

**Grip the load firmly** so that it feels secure. Your arms should be kept within the boundary formed by your legs. Bend your fingers round the load if possible. You may find that you have to change your grip during the lift, and if so you should make the changes as smoothly as possible. The heaviest side of the load should be held next to you.

**Lift smoothly**. Keep control of the load, and don't make sudden movements.

**Avoid twisting the trunk** of your body when you move to the side – move your feet instead.

**Keep the load close to your body**. Keep it close to the body for as long as possible.

**Rest the load before manoeuvring it into place**. It is usually easier to slide a load into position, rather than twisting and moving your body while holding the load.

## 6.2 Risk assessment of manual handling

On the next two pages, you can see an example of a detailed checklist that might be used when carrying out such an assessment.

Checklist forms have been taken from the HSE booklet *Manual Handling – Guidance on Regulations*.

# Activity 51 · 30 mins

**S/NVQ E6**

This Activity may provide the basis of appropriate evidence for your S/NVQ portfolio.

The checklist is taken from HSE booklet *Manual Handling – Guidance on Regulations*, and you will find it useful to have this booklet with you when you perform the Activity.

If manual handling is carried out in your workplace, use the checklist to assess a particular operation. Fill out all parts of the form, and try to come up with an overall assessment of the operation, and suggestions (if appropriate) for remedial action.

If there is no suitable operation for you to assess, you could go through a mock exercise of (say) planning the movement of a heavy box to an awkward location. Be sure to follow the guidelines for manual handling, which are more fully explained in the HSE booklet.

By all means involve your team members in this Activity, and get help if you can (perhaps from a safety officer, or your manager). You can photocopy the form if you want to, either from this workbook or from the HSE booklet.

Manual handling of loads

# ASSESSMENT CHECKLIST

| SUMMARY OF ASSESSMENT | Overall priority for remedial action: Nil/Low/Med/High (Circle as appropriate) |
|---|---|
| Operations covered by this assessment: | Remedial action to be taken: |
| _____ | _____ |
| _____ | _____ |
| _____ | _____ |
| | |
| Locations: _____ | Date by which action is to be taken: _____ |
| Personnel involved: _____ | Date for reassessment: _____ |
| _____ | Assessor's name: _____ |
| Date of assessment: _____ | Signature: _____ |

**SECTION A Preliminary**

Q1   Do the operations involve a significant risk of injury?                    YES    NO

If YES, go to Q2. If NO, the assessment need go no further. (If in doubt, answer YES.)

Q2   Can the operations be avoided/mechanized/automated at reasonable cost?   YES    NO

If NO, go to Q3. If YES, proceed and then check that the result is satisfactory.

Q3   Are the operations clearly within the guidelines?                         YES    NO

If NO, go to Section B. If YES you may go straight to Section C if you wish.

**SECTION B Detailed assessment** – see next sheet.

**SECTION C Overall assessment of risk**

Q   What is your overall assessment of the risk of injury? Insignificant/Low/Medium/High.

If not 'Insignificant' go to Section D. If 'Insignificant', the assessment need go no further.

**SECTION D Remedial Action**

Q   What remedial steps should be taken, in order of priority?

a  _____

b  _____

c  _____

d  _____

e  _____

**AND FINALLY:**

- Complete the SUMMARY above.
- Compare it with your other manual handling assessments.
- Decide your priorities for action.

TAKE ACTION – AND CHECK THAT IT HAS THE DESIRED EFFECT.

| SECTION B More detailed assessment, where necessary ||||||
| Questions to consider: (If the answer to a question is 'Yes' place a tick against it and then consider the level of risk) | Level of risk (Tick as appropriate) |||| Possible remedial action (Make rough notes in this column in preparation for completing Section D) |
| | Yes | Low | Med | High | |
| **The tasks** – do they involve:<br><br>■ holding loads away from trunk?<br>■ twisting?<br>■ stooping?<br>■ reaching upwards?<br>■ large vertical movement?<br>■ long carrying distances?<br>■ strenuous pushing or pulling?<br>■ unpredictable movement of loads?<br>■ repetitive handling?<br>■ insufficient rest or recovery?<br>■ a workrate imposed by a process? | | | | | |
| **The loads** – are they:<br><br>■ heavy?<br>■ bulky/unwieldy?<br>■ difficult to grasp?<br>■ unstable/unpredictable?<br>■ intrinsically harmful (e.g. sharp/hot?) | | | | | |
| **The working environment** – are there:<br><br>■ constraints on posture?<br>■ poor floors?<br>■ variations in levels?<br>■ hot/cold/humid conditions?<br>■ strong air movements?<br>■ poor lighting conditions? | | | | | |
| **Individual capability** – does the job:<br><br>■ require unusual capability?<br>■ hazard those with a health problem?<br>■ hazard those who are pregnant?<br>■ call for special information/training? | | | | | |
| **Other factors** –<br><br>Is movement or posture hindered by clothing or personal protective equipment? | | | | | |
| When you have completed Section B go to Section C. ||||||

# 7 Fire hazards

Fires are easily started and often difficult to control.

Your organization will by law have to provide fire extinguishers and issue instructions about what to do in case of fire.

So what more can you and your team do to reduce fire hazards and risks?

## Activity 52

Jot down some steps you think that someone in your position could take to cut down fire hazards, and the risks from fire. Try to list **four** actions. Think in terms of your own place of work.

_____

_____

_____

_____

_____

_____

The points you have listed may include some of the following. You could:

- try to minimize the quantities of flammable materials that are kept in the workplace – what is kept must be stored safely;
- make sure that staff don't create unnecessary risks by leaving flammable items about, like oil-soaked rags;
- make sure that 'No smoking' notices are obeyed;

- keep working areas and machines clean; for example, grease should be removed frequently from ducts and cooker extractors;
- make sure that, if rubbish has to be burned, it is done well away from buildings, and that fires are kept under control; extinguishers should be kept handy;
- make sure all staff know how to raise the fire alarm, and that at least some of them know how to use the extinguishers;
- ensure that no one blocks fire exits;
- never let anyone prop open fire doors.

If you use flammable liquids, gas cylinders, oxygen or other materials that present special fire risks, then you should be aware of the extra hazards, **and** know how to deal with them.

> If you need more information or advice about particular hazards, talk to the people in your organization. HSE will also supply information.

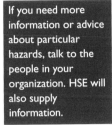

# 8 Protective equipment

Hundreds of accidents are made worse every year through workers not using adequate protective clothing and other equipment, often referred to as PPE (personal protective equipment).

Protective equipment is designed only as **a last line of defence** against hazards. Nevertheless, it can often save people from death or serious injury.

It is a legal requirement for employers to issue, and employees to use, serviceable PPE in every situation that demands it. PPE must be provided without charge to employees and they must be fully trained and instructed in its use ahead of the need to use it.

# Activity 53

3 mins

Many serious accidents occur every year in cases in which employees have been provided with the proper protective clothing, and have been told of the need for it, but don't use it.

Can you think of any reasons why employees may fail to use protective clothing, even though the clothing is available and they're aware that it should be worn? If protective clothing is used in your workplace, you may be able to draw on your own experience to answer this question.

_____

_____

_____

_____

_____

_____

_____

Some possible reasons are that they:

- feel it's 'too much trouble' to put the clothing on;
- don't really believe any hazard exists;
- may lose time (and pay) by stopping to put the clothing on;
- find the clothing awkward to use, or uncomfortable;
- know the clothing provided is defective in some way;
- believe it isn't necessary for 'just a five-minute job'.

Because protective equipment is often inconvenient, it's important to be vigilant against any tendency to do without it.

# Activity 54 · 3 mins

What steps can the first line manager take to encourage the use of proper protective clothing and equipment at all times? What steps could **you** take? Try to list **four** steps.

_____

_____

_____

_____

_____

_____

A manager or team leader can and should **firstly**, set an example at all times by using the equipment as directed:

- **identify the circumstances** when the protective equipment should be used;
- **assess** the PPE, to make certain it is suitable for the risk;
- make sure that the leader and the team are **fully trained** in its use and aware of its importance;
- make sure the protective equipment is **available**, and in good order – which means that it has to be properly **maintained**;
- make adequate provisions for the **storage** of PPE;
- ensure that every user knows **why** the equipment is necessary, and what its **limitations** are – this means, **instruction**, **information**, and **training**;
- **insist** on the use of the protective equipment and of the workteam developing the **habit** of using it;

**If protective clothing can prevent injury or illness, it should not be optional.**

- put up safety signs to **remind** people about specific protective equipment;
- **check regularly** that PPE is used, and do spot checks if necessary.

Managers and team leaders can only do so much, however. Sooner or later individuals have to take on responsibility for themselves.

Some of the various types of protection are:

| Part of body | Typical hazards | Typical equipment | Comment |
|---|---|---|---|
| Eyes | ■ flying particles;<br>■ dust;<br>■ chemical splashing;<br>■ flying molten metal;<br>■ vapours and gases;<br>■ infectious materials;<br>■ radiation. | Spectacles, goggles, helmets and face screens. | Eye protection to an approved specification must be used for some processes. You should make sure you know whether this is the case with the processes you and your staff work with. |
| Hearing | ■ Noise. | Muffs or earplugs – but choose with care, as many are ineffective. | Hearing is susceptible to many kinds of noise. Extremely loud noise is dangerous even for brief exposures. |
| Head and neck | ■ falling objects;<br>■ hair entanglement;<br>■ chemical splashing;<br>■ working in extreme climates or temperatures. | Hats, caps, helmets, hairnets, hoods and skullcaps. | As with all equipment, the type of headgear must be effective against the known hazards. |
| Hands and arms | ■ cuts by anything sharp – even by a sheet of paper in an office;<br>■ burns;<br>■ crushing;<br>■ contamination by infectious materials;<br>■ splashing with chemicals;<br>■ electric shocks;<br>■ being hit by moving objects;<br>■ abrasions. | Gloves, mitts, armlets, chainmail gloves. | Gloves intended for protection against sharp objects may be very poor protection against some chemicals.<br><br>But if gloves reduce the ability to grip, or if the edges of the gloves might catch in a machine, it could be safer not to wear them. |
| Feet and legs | ■ slipping;<br>■ cuts and abrasions;<br>■ punctures (e.g. stepping on a nail);<br>■ falling objects;<br>■ heavy pressures;<br>■ chemical and metal splashing;<br>■ wet surfaces;<br>■ electrostatic build-up. | Safety boots with steel toe-caps, reinforced shoes, gaiters and leggings, knee-pads. | |
| Body | ■ heat, cold and bad climatic conditions;<br>■ chemical and metal splashing;<br>■ spray from pressure leaks or spray guns;<br>■ impact. | Coats, aprons, jackets, boiler suits, high visibility clothing. | Materials may be anti-static, non-flammable, chain mail, chemically impermeable and insulated (against heat or cold), and so on. |

# 9 Day-to-day tasks

As a manager, you have a responsibility for the general condition of your immediate working environment.

## 9.1 Housekeeping

In any workplace, housekeeping – that is, general organization, cleanliness, tidiness and maintenance – plays an important role in helping to prevent accidents.

Give an example of an accident that might be prevented through good housekeeping.

_____

_____

_____

_____

Some of the hazards that may lurk in any workplace, which can be easily spotted, and can often be eliminated by simple housekeeping, are:

- articles left on the floor, which may trip the unwary;
- slippery floors, as a result of being wet, or incorrectly polished;
- clutter, which makes people bump into things or fall over;
- sharp corners on furniture, which might injure passers-by;
- items stored at above head height, with no proper provision for getting them down without over-stretching;
- tools left lying about that may be sharp or otherwise dangerous;
- blocked gangways, or a badly designed layout, leading people into hazards in their efforts to get past;
- build up of flammable waste materials that could provide fuel for a fire.

These are just some of the more common hazards. You may have thought of other ways that accidents might be caused.

Apart from helping to eradicate particular hazards, good housekeeping can have a positive effect on the quality and standards of work and behaviour. When employees see high standards being set, they tend to follow them.

If you work in a shop or some other place used by members of the public, then it is even more important to take care of the premises.

# 9.2 Stress

But there are other factors, besides housekeeping, that can increase the risk of accidents in the local environment. These include:

- poor lighting;
- high levels of noise;
- too much or too little heat;
- inadequate ventilation;
- the effects of chemicals.

Of course, besides being unpleasant and unhealthy, most of these can be hazardous in themselves. Sustained high noise levels, for example, can cause ear damage, and people die from lack of air. But even when they have no immediate or direct effects, these factors often result in **stress.**

It's a known fact that stress helps to cause accidents. Even when they are simply uncomfortable, through having to wear unsuitable clothing for example, people are more likely to lose their temper and be irritable. This irritability can result in a lack of control over movement and action, which in turn can increase the likelihood of an accident.

Activity 56

2 mins

Apart from their physical environment, can you think of **one** other factor which may result in increased stress in people at work? Thinking about your own workplace may help you answer this.

_____

_____

_____

You may have answered:

- too much work;
- difficult relationships with colleagues or superiors;
- lack of training;
- lack of information.

There are any number of things that put people under stress.

As a manager or team leader, you will need to take account of causes and symptoms of stress, if you want to reduce the risk of accidents.

**Anyone under stress is more likely to have an accident.**

One very important cause, and result, of stress is **fatigue**. That's why rest and meal breaks are important.

To sum up this section, the lessons to be learned are that:

- working areas should be kept clean, tidy and well maintained;
- good housekeeping prevents accidents;
- discomfort and fatigue increase stress, and stress causes accidents;
- signs of stress among your team should be taken seriously.

## Activity 57 · 15 mins

S/NVQ E6

This Activity may provide the basis of appropriate evidence for your S/NVQ portfolio. If you are intending to take this course of action, it might be better to write your answers on separate sheets of paper.

Look back through this session, and select one of the areas covered that is applicable to your own situation: equipment safety; preventing falls; electrical hazards; maintenance; fire hazards; protective equipment; or day-to-day hazards. (You should already have completed Activity 51 on manual handling.)

Undertake a thorough review of the accident prevention measures currently in place in your work area, in respect of your chosen topic. You can use the points listed in this session as a checklist, or you may want to make up your own checklist, based on experience or on another document.

Get your team involved in this exercise if possible, and don't be afraid to ask for help from your colleagues.

# Self-assessment 5

*15 mins*

1 The following statements have been split in half. Match the correct second half with each first half.

| | | | |
|---|---|---|---|
| a | Accident prevention shouldn't depend on | i | just good practice – it's the law. |
| b | Ensure that young persons are | ii | people always obeying the rules. |
| c | Inspection and maintenance of | iii | unguarded machines, may be against the law. |
| d | It's useful to think about | iv | equipment are essential. |
| e | Keep untrained and | v | well marked and easily accessible. |
| f | Keeping the guards in place is not | vi | protect non-employees. |
| g | Equipment that hasn't been in use | vii | unauthorized people away from dangerous machines. |
| h | Organizations have a duty to | viii | should be checked. |
| I | Switches should be | ix | trained and supervised. |
| j | Using untrained operators, or | x | what might go wrong. |

2 What are the **two** most important points to bear in mind about good housekeeping?

_____

_____

_____

_____

3 List **three** ways of reducing the risk from electric shock.

_____

_____

_____

_____

4    What are the **three** kinds of falls that most commonly occur in workplaces?

_____

_____

_____

_____

5    List **four** precautions you might take to help prevent a ladder accident.

_____

_____

_____

_____

The answers to these questions can be found on pages 179–80.

# 10 Summary

- In accident prevention, it's useful to think about what **might** go wrong. Make plans on the assumption that what could go wrong, will go wrong.

- Accident prevention **shouldn't depend** on people always obeying the rules.

- When dealing with equipment safety:

  - keeping the guards in place is not just good practice – it's the law;
  - inspection and maintenance of equipment are essential;
  - keep untrained and unauthorized people away;
  - switches should be well marked and easily accessible;
  - equipment that hasn't been in use must be checked;
  - ensure that young persons are trained and supervised: using untrained operators, or unguarded machines, may be against the law.

- To prevent **falls** at the same level, some of the points mentioned were to:

  - check surfaces, to ensure they're in good repair;
  - put up barriers to prevent people walking on temporarily wet and slippery floors;
  - keep areas where people walk well lit;
  - keep surfaces free from clutter;
  - don't allow running or 'larking about';
  - permit no intoxication, under any circumstances.

- To prevent people **falling from one level to another**, ensure that:

  - openings are guarded, well marked and well lit;
  - covers can withstand any expected load or impact;
  - covers are clearly identified.

- To prevent **falls from ladders**:

  - secure ladders by tying at the top, or else at the sides or bottom;
  - don't allow anyone to work on a ladder without a handhold;
  - check to see that ladders are not weak or damaged;
  - place ladder at a slope of four units up to one out from the base;
  - do not place a ladder against a fragile surface, such as a plastic gutter;
  - make sure the ladder is placed on an secure footing;
  - use the correct ladder for the job.

- **Roof workers** should:

  - never make assumptions about the strength of materials;
  - always use proper equipment;
  - never ignore hazards.

- To protect against being hurt by **falling objects**:

  - don't walk under loads that are suspended, such as from a crane;
  - don't throw anything down from above; get it lowered safely;
  - always wear protective clothing such as helmets and safety shoes where there is a hazard of falling objects.
  - don't leave tools near to the edge of surfaces, or in an unstable position;
  - use isolation barriers where there is a hazard of falling objects.

- For **electrical safety**:

  - no-one should be allowed to open covers which give access to live electrical parts, unless they are fully trained and competent to do so;
  - there should be a well-marked switch or isolator close to every machine;
  - all electrical installations to be checked regularly by a trained electrician;
  - workteams should be trained to make sure that tools and power sockets are switched off before plugging them in.

- For **maintenance safety**:

  - explain precisely what the condition of the plant or machinery is, as far as you are able to determine;
  - tell the maintenance staff how to isolate the plant or machinery;
  - provide appropriate safety equipment, including first aid materials, and explain how emergency help can be obtained;
  - discuss the condition of the equipment with the maintenance staff, before attempting to put it back into service;
  - check whether a permit to work is required.

- Before any **manual handling** is done, you will need to stand back and think about the task, and the possible alternatives. Is manual handling really necessary?

- **Training** should be given in correct handling techniques.

- To protect against **fire hazards**:

  - make sure that 'No Smoking' notices are obeyed;
  - keep working areas and machines clean; for example, grease should be removed frequently from ducts and cooker extractors;
  - make sure that, if rubbish has to be burned, it should be done well away from buildings, and fires kept under control; extinguishers should be kept handy;
  - make sure all staff know how to raise the fire alarm, and that at least some of them know how to use the extinguishers;
  - ensure that no one blocks fire exits or props open fire doors.

■   With regard to **personal protective equipment (PPE)**:

- ■  set an example at all times by using the PPE as directed;
- ■  identify the circumstances when the PPE should be used;
- ■  assess the PPE, to make certain it is suitable for the risk;
- ■  make sure the team are fully trained in its use and aware of its importance;
- ■  make sure the PPE is available, and in good order;
- ■  make adequate provisions for the storage;
- ■  provide instruction, information and training;
- ■  insist on the use of the protective equipment and of the workteam developing the habit of using it;
- ■  check regularly that PPE is used, and carry out spot checks if necessary.

■   In any workplace, **housekeeping** – that is, general organization, cleanliness, tidiness and maintenance – plays an important role in helping to prevent accidents, and can have a positive effect on the quality and standards of work and behaviour.

■   Anyone under **stress** is more likely to have an accident.

# Session F
# Coping with accidents

## 1 Introduction

Though most accidents are preventable, it's a fact of life that accidents do happen, whatever we do to try to prevent them. When they occur, there is more work for the first line manager to do.

For one thing, you need to be prepared for the worst, and to train people in dealing with emergencies.

Then, after it's over, an accident has to be reported, and perhaps investigated.

## 2 Dealing with accidents and abnormal occurrences

It may well be part of your job to handle things in an emergency at work. How would you go about it?

Let's first list some of the accidents and emergencies which might occur in a place of work.

# Activity 58

Think about your own place of work. Jot down **two** or **three** examples of any accidents which you know have occurred in the past.

_____

_____

_____

_____

_____

_____

Now try to think of situations where an accident came close to occurring – perhaps someone fell but wasn't injured, or someone didn't bother to wear protective clothing when they should have, but 'got away with it'.

_____

_____

_____

_____

_____

Depending on the type of activity which takes place and the circumstances, some or all of the following are possible:

- a fire;
- an explosion;
- electric shock;
- someone falling, or something falling on someone;
- a flood;
- a release of dangerous gases;
- a poisoning;
- a release of radioactivity;
- someone being hurt or trapped by a machine;
- someone getting burned;
- a road or other transport accident;

You may have thought of (or have heard about) other kinds of accidents. The list of things that might possibly go wrong is bound to be a long one.

Your company may well have written instructions as to what people should do in the event of an accident. There will certainly be fire instructions, and there should be instructions for dealing with accidents arising from any special risks involved in the different areas of work.

## Activity 59

Instructions that tell people what to do in the event of an emergency would normally include, for example:

■ saying what might happen, and how an alarm would be raised.

Try to locate any emergency instructions that are displayed at your place of work, and, having read the wording carefully, try to list two further points that emergency instructions might include.

_____

_____

_____

_____

_____

_____

_____

You may have listed any of the following:

■ role of fire marshals, accounting for staff, visitors and customers;
■ how to call the emergency services;
■ how to reach safety;
■ who should be informed of the situation;
■ where to find rescue equipment;
■ saying what might happen, and how an alarm would be raised;
■ the names or titles of people who would take charge in the event of an incident;
■ where to find first aid equipment, and the names of people who are trained in giving first aid;
■ how to shut down plant or make equipment safe.

First line managers are expected to take a lead in implementing safety arrangements. You may want to give some thought to whether your team members are sufficiently well informed about how to deal with emergencies.

Now let's look at what should be done when an emergency does occur.

In the following activities, imagine that you arrive at the scene **immediately** after each incident has happened.

## Activity 60

### Situation 1

Two workmen are painting at the top of some scaffolding. The scaffolding suddenly collapses and the men are thrown to the ground. They appear to be seriously injured.

You arrive at the scene. What do you do?

_____

_____

_____

_____

_____

_____

_____

_____

The first thing you would have to do is to assess the situation. An important step is to establish whether further harm or damage could yet occur. For example, part of the scaffolding may still be liable to fall. It may not be easy to decide whether the area is safe.

■ The most sensible first step in a situation like this is therefore to make sure no one else could get hurt, including yourself. You may need to clear the area.

■ You may need to organize other potential helpers in the vicinity, and you would certainly need to call for medical help, perhaps by telling someone to telephone for an ambulance.

■ First aid must be given to the injured as soon as possible.

This was an example of a serious accident, and one which would have to be reported, both within the organization, and to the HSE. We will discuss reporting shortly.

## Activity 61

3 mins

### Situation 2

A tank containing poisonous and flammable liquid ruptures and begins spraying the surrounding area, soaking the clothes of two operators nearby.

You arrive at the scene and assess what has happened. What do you do?

_____

_____

_____

_____

_____

_____

_____

The liquid may well be giving off toxic or asphyxiating fumes, and may be absorbed into clothing. There is also a risk of fire, so this is a very hazardous situation to deal with. A difficult rescue operation may have to be mounted.

■ Your first thought, again, must be to prevent the accident becoming worse than it already is. In a number of accidents of this kind, would-be rescuers have become additional victims, as in this example.

> **Example**
>
> A road tanker was carrying a load of oleum (fuming sulphuric acid) along the M6 motorway. The weather was foggy and, as the driver was taking avoiding action, he swerved and struck the nearside of a stationary container lorry. The collision was sufficiently violent to rupture the tank and some 13 tons of oleum was spilt on to the road. A woman driving a following car stopped near the crash and got out of her car. She slipped and fell into a pool of acid and was burned so severely that she subsequently died; twenty other people also suffered acid burns in the incident.[1]

- Getting expert medical and fire service help is essential, and you will need to describe what has happened. The emergency services – the fire and ambulance crews – will want to know what the liquid is. (This information will be displayed on the tank in the form of a code, whether a road tanker or a fixed tank is involved.)
- As soon as possible, the affected operators must be taken to a safe area and given medical help. Removing clothing may be a priority.

Again, this accident would have to be reported.

# Activity 62

3 mins

## Situation 3

Through faulty electrical wiring, a power tool becomes 'live', giving a severe electric shock to the person using it. The tool then falls onto a metal bench.

You arrive at the scene. What do you do?

_____

_____

_____

_____

_____

[1] Text from Health and Safety Commission Newsletter, April 1987.

The same general approach should be applied.

1 Assess the situation.

2 Make the area safe: in this case the first thing to be done is to switch off the power.

3 Get someone to call expert help: urgent medical help would be needed.

4 If you are qualified, apply first aid to the injured. In a case like this, every second will count.

Unless you are trained in dealing with the kind of emergency described in each incident above, you may feel that you couldn't cope. Although you may not be confident in knowing exactly what to do in a particular situation, there are rules which apply to **any** emergency.

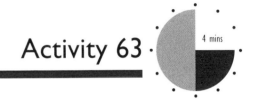

Activity 63 · 4 mins

Based on the answers to the three incidents above, summarize what should be done in the event of any emergency, by listing **three** or **four** points.

_____

_____

_____

_____

_____

_____

The actions you should have listed, in your own words, are:

■ Assess the situation

to see what actions are needed.

■ Make the area safe

so that no one else is in danger. If this isn't possible, clear everyone away from the area. Make sure there will be no additional victims.

■ Get help

from any appropriate source: colleagues, the Ambulance Service, the Fire Service, and/or the Police.

■ Give first aid

to any people injured. If necessary, call for medical assistance.

Once the emergency is under control, there are still more actions to be taken.

## Activity 64

What further steps should be taken after an accident, once the immediate emergency has been dealt with?

_____

_____

_____

_____

_____

_____

_____

_____

If the accident is to be investigated, **nothing should be moved unnecessarily**. For example, in the case of the accident with the scaffolding, you shouldn't allow anyone to start dismantling the structure, beyond making it safe. Doing this could destroy evidence about the cause of the accident.

With any accident; the names and addresses of any witnesses should be taken.

Also, **the accident has to be reported**. We'll look at the matter of reporting next.

# 3 Reporting accidents

Some accidents must be reported as a legal requirement.

Unfortunately, accidents don't always get reported. If it were possible to ask people involved in accidents why they didn't report them, you would probably get answers like:

- 'I didn't think it was serious enough. No-one was seriously hurt.'
- 'Last time this happened I filled out the accident form as I was told. But nothing happened – no one took any notice.'
- 'I haven't got time to sit around filling out forms. I've got important work to do.'
- 'I don't want to get involved. I don't want to tell tales about my mates'

## Activity 65 · 3 mins

Why do you think it is so important to report accidents? Try to give **two** reasons.

_____

_____

_____

_____

Some reasons are as follows.

- To help to prevent further accidents.

When an accident is reported within an organization, an investigation can be mounted, which may well result in new safety measures being introduced to prevent recurrences. To do this effectively, it is essential to collect data on **all accidents**, including 'non-injury' ones and 'near misses' too.

■ To enable compensation claims to be made.

If an accident at work is not reported as having occurred as soon as it happens, it may be very difficult to prove at a later stage that it actually did, especially if the effects of the accident don't become obvious for some time afterwards. Furthermore, when a claim for compensation is made, it is vital that it be established that the injury occurred at work.

■ So that special precautions can be taken.

A survey of reported accidents may well reveal unsuspected risks or adverse conditions, and so on. The organization can then concentrate on how to prevent related accidents from occurring in the future.

---

**POINT OF LAW**

The Reporting of Injuries, Diseases and Dangerous Occurrences (RIDDOR) Regulations require organizations to notify the relevant enforcement authority (the HSE) 'by the quickest practicable means' – usually by telephone. Subsequently a report must be made within ten days on the approved form in the event of:

■ the **death** of any person as a result of an accident arising out of or in connection with work;
■ any person at work suffering a **specified major injury** as a result of an accident arising out of or in connection with work;
■ any person who is not at work suffering an injury as a result of an accident arising out of or in connection with work, and where that person is taken from the site of the accident to a hospital for treatment in respect of that injury;
■ any person who is not at work suffering a major injury as a result of an accident arising out of or in connection with **work at a hospital;**
■ where there is a **dangerous occurrence**.

A report must also be made as soon as practicable, and in any event within ten days of the accident, where anyone is **incapacitated for work** that he or she might reasonably be expected to do, **for more than three consecutive days**. The report has to be made even if the injured person is not away from work but, for example, performing light duties.

---

It is part of a manager's job to make sure **all** accidents get reported. Other staff may look to the manager, too, to do everything possible to make sure the same accident can't happen again.

Filling out an accident form and then locking it away in a filing cabinet and forgetting about it will do no one any good at all.

# 4 Investigating an accident

As part of a sound system of safety, organizations should investigate the direct and indirect causes behind accidents at work.

The investigators would want to know a number of things, including:

- what type of accident it was, such as a maintenance accident, a trip or a fall and so on;
- what injuries, if any, were inflicted;
- whether the law was broken;
- whether the accident is a notifiable one;
- if an insurance claim should be made.

Investigations should begin as soon as practicable, following the occurrence. The more time that passes, the more likelihood there is of the people involved forgetting the details, or of physical evidence being destroyed.

## 4.1 Who investigates?

Who should take part in running an investigation?

Activity 66 · 3 mins

Who would you expect to participate in managing an accident investigation in your organization?

_____

_____

_____

Usually, the question regarding which people take part will depend on the seriousness of the incident. You may be asked to run an investigation, if something happens in your own work area. Alternatively, a more senior colleague, or a safety officer, may take charge. Trade union representatives are normally also invited to participate.

If the accident is a serious one, the HSE may decide to carry out their own investigation. Lawyers representing injured persons, and/or insurance assessors, may also need to be involved.

## 4.2 What do they do?

The following procedure covers most points of an investigation. The investigator's job will involve some or all of the following:

- **Find out the facts**, regarding:

  - the sequence of events that led up to the accident;
  - the system of work in operation;
  - environmental factors;
  - the plant and equipment involved;
  - the people who were present.

- **Take photographs**, make sketches, and take measurements of the scene and the relevant features. Later, scaled drawings may have to be produced.

- **Obtain statements**, as soon as possible, from all persons who were involved in, or who observed, the accident. Write down their names and addresses, who they work for, and the reasons they were on the site. For a serious occurrence, interviews should ideally be recorded, and/or take place in front of a third party.

- **Review the facts**, in the light of what has been learned, taking steps to resolve any inconsistencies or conflicting evidence.

- **Get expert help**, if necessary: for example, to examine machinery.

> It is *not* the purpose of an investigation to find somebody to blame for the accident.

- **Come to a conclusion**, if possible, regarding the causes of the accident.

- **Generate a written report** of the accident, which describes what happened, sets out the causes, and recommends changes to prevent a recurrence.

# 4.3 What happens next?

As a result of the investigation, action needs to be taken, to prevent a further accident. Some of the following questions will have to be answered. Should:

- further investigation take place?
- new instructions be implemented?
- further training take place?
- new system of work – such as a permit to work system – be installed?
- the job be analysed, to find out whether it should be done in a different way?
- different materials be used?
- different work methods be used?
- the work be done in a different place or environment?
- the work be supervised more closely?
- responsibilities be reassigned?
- expert advice be sought?
- information may be made available to other sites that operate in similar circumstances, use similar plant or that in other ways might benefit from the results of the specific investigation? (Many industries have systems established to do this, but not all.)

# Self-assessment 6

1  What immediate actions should be taken at the scene of any accident?

a  _____

_____

b  _____

_____

c  _____

_____

d  _____

_____

2  List **five** important actions for someone investigating an accident.

_____

_____

_____

_____

_____

_____

_____

_____

_____

_____

The answers to these questions can be found on pages 180–81.

# 5 Summary

- **Many kinds** of **unexpected accidents** and incidents may occur, and people in the workplace have to know how to deal with them.

- When an **emergency** occurs, the following steps should be followed:

  1 **Assess the situation**, to see what actions are needed.
  2 **Make the area safe**, so that no one else is in danger. If this isn't possible, clear everyone away from the area. Make sure there will be no additional victims.
  3 **Get help** from any appropriate authority: colleagues, the Ambulance Service, the Fire Service, the Police – whichever is appropriate.
  4 **Give first aid** to any people injured. If necessary, call for medical assistance.

- Accidents must be **reported**:
  - to help to prevent further accidents;
  - to enable compensation claims to be made;
  - so that special precautions can be taken;
  - for legal reasons.

- **Accident investigators** should find out:
  - what sequence of events led up to the accident;
  - what system of work was in operation;
  - about any relevant environmental factors;
  - what plant and equipment was involved;
  - who was present.

- The investigators should also:
  - take photographs, make sketches, and take measurements of the scene and the relevant features;
  - obtain statements, as soon as possible, from all persons who were involved in, or who observed, the accident;
  - review the facts, in the light of what has been learned, taking steps to resolve any inconsistencies or conflicting evidence;
  - get expert help, if necessary;
  - come to a conclusion, if possible, regarding the causes of the accident;
  - generate a written report of the accident, which describes what happened, sets out the causes, and recommends changes to prevent a recurrence;
  - make the information available to other sites that operate in similar circumstances or use similar equipment.

# Performance
# checks

Jot down the answers to the following questions on *Managing Health and Safety at Work*:

Question 1   What do you understand by the term 'enabling law'? Give two examples.

_____

_____

_____

Question 2   What are the **three** routes by which an organization might have a legal action brought against it, as a result of an accident at work?

_____

_____

_____

Question 3   When a Directive is issued by the EU, what actions are taken by member States?

_____

_____

Question 4   One thing an employer must do, in order to comply with **HSWA**, is to ensure plant and equipment are safely installed, operated and maintained. Give **two** other examples of what it must do.

_____

_____

Question 5    How would you summarize the responsibilities of employees under HSWA?

_____

_____

Question 6    If a regulation uses the words 'the employer shall', how should that be interpreted?

_____

_____

Question 7    How would you explain what it means to carry out a risk assessment, in a sentence or two?

_____

_____

Question 8    Briefly, what is the purpose of health surveillance?

_____

_____

Question 9    How would you define a 'competent person' who is to help an employer comply with health and safety laws?

_____

_____

Question 10   Which **two** sets of regulations are important in respect of workstations?

_____

_____

Question 11   What's the first thing you should consider, if you plan to move a heavy load manually?

_____

_____

Question 12   List **two** requirements for employers under the Personal Protective Equipment at Work Regulations 1992 (PPEWR).

_____

_____

Question 13   How would you define a hazardous substance, under COSHH 2?

_____

_____

Question 14   Why is it important to learn lessons from incidents in which nobody gets hurt and no damage is done?

_____

_____

Question 15   What is meant by the statement 'accidents at work are largely caused by poor control and management of safety'?

_____

_____

Question 16   Why is it important for organizations to set safety standards that are measurable, and against which objectives can be compared?

_____

_____

Question 17   What is meant by the expression 'the accident iceberg of costs'?

_____

_____

Question 18   Why must safety strategies in organizations be proactive, rather than reactive?

_____

_____

Question 19   Which are the **three** principal sources of law for health and safety?

_____

_____

_____

Question 20   Briefly summarize an employee's duties under the Health and Safety at Work, etc. Act 1974.

_____

_____

Question 21    Define, in your own words, what risk assessment is.

_____

_____

Question 22    Write down **four** appropriate actions to help prevent accidents on ladders.

_____

_____

_____

_____

Question 23    Why is static electricity sometimes dangerous?

_____

_____

Question 24    Write down **three** questions that you should ask **before** asking people to move heavy loads manually.

_____

_____

_____

Question 25    Note down **four** kinds of hazard that might result in injury to the eyes.

_____

_____

_____

_____

Question 26    Explain briefly why good housekeeping helps accident prevention.

_____

_____

Question 27 What simple advice would you give a manager who is trying to plan for emergencies, and is trying to work out what kind of abnormal occurrences are likely to take place?

_____

_____

Question 28 What are the **four** actions to be performed, in the event of any emergency?

_____

_____

_____

Answers to these questions can be found on page 181.

# 2 Workbook assessment

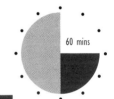

60 mins

Read the following case incident and then deal with the instruction that follows. Write your answers on a separate sheet of paper.

John Cardiff and Sharon Newton work as Team Leaders (John in Administration; Sharon in Goods Receipt) for a cash and carry warehouse owned by a local businessman. A Health and Safety Committee is to be formed at the site. This followed the appointment of a part-time Safety Advisor, after a nasty accident involving a goods lift, which injured two employees badly. The General Manager will chair the first meeting and will be hard to convince that real changes need to be made, whatever the owner, who is not involved in day-to-day management, thinks.

John and Sharon have both offered to serve on the Committee. From talking to their colleagues, they are concerned that the first meeting may be spoiled by recriminations and turn into a 'bitching session'. There is also a feeling amongst staff that in future 'Safety is down to the new Safety Advisor – it's nothing to do with us'.

Both Team Leaders want the new committee to help improve safety around the site. Their concerns include offices, general areas such as car parks, staff rest areas and the way that outside contractors (for building and cleaning work) behave. They know of several 'near misses' which have happened, two involving customers and yet another goods lift incident during an evening shift.

Please put yourself in the position of the two Team Leaders. Develop a list of recommendations that they should make to the General Manager and their colleagues on the Safety Committee. They should aim to convince them that the committee can and must act to help prevent accidents happening in the future.

Referring both to this Workbook and your own experience at work, make a case for improvement on

- moral
- legal
- commercial grounds.

Specify any assumptions you have made about the accident and 'near miss' record of the firm. Justify each of your recommendations clearly, so that someone less familiar with the subject than you are will be able to follow your reasoning. Try to write no more than a page or so in total.

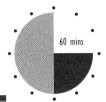

60 mins

# 3 Work-based assignment

S/NVQ
E6

The time guide for this assignment gives you an approximate idea of how long it is likely to take you to write up your findings. You will find you need to spend some additional time gathering information, talking to colleagues, and thinking about the assignment.

Your written response to this assignment may form useful evidence for your S/NVQ portfolio.

**What you have to do**

Identify a hazard within your own work environment, that might lead to an accident. Describe what this hazard consists of. Then co-operate with your team to carry out a risk assessment, by estimating:

- the likelihood or probability that an accident might occur as a result of the hazard;
- how serious the outcome might be, if it did occur;
- how often the risk is present.

Do not make snap judgements: all these questions require a good deal of thought. You may not feel you have enough experience or knowledge to complete this exercise on your own, so by all means call upon the expertise of colleagues, including any with specific training in risk assessment.

You may decide to calculate a risk rating, using the tables listed in Session D or using a method adopted by your organization. However, the important outcome of this assessment is to determine precisely what actions you recommend taking, in order to eliminate or reduce the risk.

Write your response in the form of a report to your manager.

# Reflect and review

## 1 Reflect and review

Now that you have completed your work on *Managing Health and Safety at Work*, let us review our workbook objectives.

The first objective was:

■ When you have completed this workbook you will be better able to identify the most important laws related to health and safety.

We have covered a lot of ground in this workbook: many different statutes related to health and safety were reviewed. These are the laws that are currently the most important to work organizations generally.

■ What can you do to increase your knowledge of health and safety law?

_____

_____

The second objective was:

■ When you have completed this workbook you will be better able to find out more about laws that are especially relevant to the work you do.

If you followed the workbook carefully, you should now have at least some idea about the kind of laws that deal with your type of work and organization. Now's the time to follow these up.

■ Write down the laws that you know about, that are particularly relevant to your work.

_____

_____

_____

_____

_____

_____

_____

_____

■ Now write down the actions you plan to take to find out more about these and (perhaps) other laws.

_____

_____

_____

_____

_____

_____

_____

_____

The third objective was:

■ When you have completed this workbook you will be better able to explain to your team how the law affects them, and the duties imposed by the law on everyone at work.

A good starting point would be the Health and Safety at Work, etc. Act 1974, which makes specific reference to employees' duties. Then you should consider the other 'six-pack' regulations, and COSHH if relevant, all of which we covered in Session B.

■ Are you clear in your own mind about these laws, at least so far as to be able to pass on the relevant information?

_____

_____

■ If you are still confused about the law, what steps do you intend to take to clarify your thinking on the subject?

_____

_____

■ If your team is in need of further information and training on health and safety, what plans will you make for them to receive it?

_____

_____

The fourth objective was:

■ When you have completed this workbook you will be better able to play your part in implementing and maintaining safe systems of work.

A safe system of work was defined as 'the integration of people, machinery and materials in a correct working environment to provide the safest possible working conditions'. Systems are derived from organizational policies, and, to some extent, your scope in implementing safe systems will depend on the structures in place. However, there is plenty to be done at a local level.

■ Write down **one** way in which you could improve your team's working conditions, to make them safer:

_____

_____

_____

_____

■ How will you put measures in place to do this?

_____

_____

_____

_____

■ Is your team's working environment safer or more hazardous than it was six months ago? If it is more hazardous, what plans do you intend to make to get them back to the earlier level of safety?

_____

_____

_____

_____

The fifth objective was:

■ When you have completed this workbook you will be better able to identify hazards in your workplace, and take effective precautions against them.

We have discussed a number of hazards, including some that helped to cause the seven 'classic' accident types. Hazards exist everywhere: in offices, factories, hospitals, schools, on the road – in all environments that people work. Identifying hazards is a key task of any first line manager, and you will no doubt want to encourage your team in being vigilant in this regard.

■ How can you become more systematic in your identification of hazards in your work area?

_____

_____

_____

■ How can you improve the precautions already in place?

_____

_____

_____

The sixth objective was:

■ When you have completed this workbook you will be better able to take part in risk assessment.

As a representative of your employer, you have to play your part in assessing the risks to the health and safety of your team to which they are exposed at work, and the risks to the health and safety of visitors and others. We defined risk assessment as:

**'an identification of the hazards present in an undertaking and an estimate of the extent of the risks involved, taking into account whatever precautions are already being taken'.**

This is an important new responsibility, placed on employers by the law. Every organization must carry out risk assessments. We discussed the fact that three aspects of hazards must be evaluated:

■ the likelihood or probability that an accident might occur;
■ how serious the outcome might be, if it did occur;
■ how often the risk is present.

This obligation means more than carrying out a single exercise. Because new hazards are always appearing, and the level of risk is typically changing frequently, risk assessment must be repeated over and over.

■ Have all the hazards in your work environment been assessed recently?

_____

_____

_____

■ How can you learn more about the process of risk assessment?

_____

_____

_____

The next objective of the workbook was:

■ When you have completed this workbook you will be better able to identify some important points of health and safety law.

The law on health and safety is embodied in many Acts and Regulations. In this workbook, we have covered only some of them, notably the Health and Safety at Work, etc. Act 1974, and the Management of Health and Safety at Work Regulations 1999.

■ How can you learn more about the law on health and safety?

_____

_____

_____

The final objective was:

■ When you have completed this workbook you will be better able to cope with, report on and investigate accidents at work.

Session F dealt with these three topics. We noted that there is a procedure that can be applied to all abnormal occurrences and emergencies. The reporting of accidents is important, in order to:

■ help to prevent further accidents;
■ enable compensation claims to be made;
■ allow special precautions to be taken;
■ comply with the law.

Accident investigators want to know:

- what type of accident it was, such as a maintenance accident, a trip or a fall, and so on;
- what injuries, if any, were inflicted;
- whether the law was broken;
- if an insurance claim should be made.

- Are you confident that you can handle most emergencies? If not, what do you need to do to become more confident?

_____

_____

_____

- How could you improve your accident reporting procedures?

_____

_____

_____

- How can you find out more about accident investigation?

_____

_____

_____

# 2 Action plan

Use this plan to further develop for yourself a course of action you want to take. Make a note in the left-hand column of the issues or problems you want to tackle, and then decide what you intend to do, and make a note in column 2.

The resources you need might include time, materials, information or money. You may need to negotiate for some of them, but they could be something easily acquired, like half an hour of somebody's time, or a chapter of a book. Put whatever you need in column 3. No plan means anything without a timescale, so put a realistic target completion date in column 4.

Finally, describe the outcome you want to achieve as a result of this plan, whether it is for your own benefit or advancement, or a more efficient way of doing things.

Desired outcomes

| 1 Issues | 2 Action | 3 Resources | 4 Target completion |
|----------|----------|-------------|---------------------|
|          |          |             |                     |

Actual outcomes

# 3 Extensions

| Extension 1 | Book | *Health and Safety Law* |
|---|---|---|
| | Author | Jeremy Stranks |
| | Edition | 4th edition 2001 |
| | Publisher | Prentice Hall |

**Extension 2**

Book — *Workplace health, safety and welfare: a short guide for managers*
Edition — 1997
Publisher — HSE Books
Available from the HSE website: www.hsebooks.co.uk

**Extension 3**

Book — *Successful health and safety management*
Edition — 1997
Publisher — HSE Books
Available from the HSE website: www.hsebooks.co.uk

**Extension 4**

Book — *Safety representatives and safety committees*
Edition — 1996
Publisher — HSE Books
Available from the HSE website: www.hsebooks.co.uk

**Extension 5**

Book — *Management of Health and Safety at Work Regulations 1999 Approved Code of Practice and guidance*
Edition — 2000
Publisher — HSE Books
Available from the HSE website: www.hsebooks.co.uk

**Extension 6**

Book — *Manual Handling Operations Regulations 1999*
Edition — 1998
Publisher — HSE Books
Available from the HSE website: www.hsebooks.co.uk

**Extension 7**

Book — *VDUs: an easy guide to the Regulations. How to comply with the Health and Safety (display screen equipment) Regulations 1992*
Edition — 1997
Publisher — HSE Books
Available from the HSE website: www.hsebooks.co.uk

**Extension 8**          COMPANY _____

## HEALTH & SAFETY DATA RECORD

SECTION 1 – PRODUCT IDENTIFICATION

| | |
|---|---|
| **TRADE NAME/CHEMICAL NAME** | |
| **APPROX. ANNUAL CONSUMPTION** | |
| **SUPPLIER/MANUFACTURER** | |
| **STORAGE AREA** | |
| **POINT (S) OF USE** | |

SECTION 2 – HAZARDOUS INGREDIENTS

| | |
|---|---|
| **MATERIAL OR COMPONENT** | |

SECTION 3 – PHYSICAL PROPERTIES

| | | |
|---|---|---|
| **APPEARANCE AND COLOUR** | | |
| **SPECIFIC GRAVITY ($H_2O = 1$)** | **SOLUBILITY IN WATER:** | |
| **BULK DENSITY:** | **VISCOSITY AT:** | **pH 1% SOLN:** |

SECTION 4 – FLAMMABILITY & EXPLOSIVE PROPERTIES

| | |
|---|---|
| **FLASH POINT (TEST METHOD)** | |
| **EXTINGUISHING MEDIA** | |
| **SPECIAL FIRE FIGHTING PROCEDURES** | |
| **UNUSUAL FIRE & EXPLOSION HAZARD** | |

SECTION 5 – HEALTH HAZARD DATA    REPORT *ALL* ACCIDENTS TO THE SURGERY

| | |
|---|---|
| **THRESHOLD LIMIT VALUE** | |
| **EFFECTS OF EXPOSURE** | |
| **EMERGENCY FIRST AID PROCEDURES**<br>**EYES:**<br>**SKIN:**<br>**INGESTION:**<br>**INHALATION:** | |

SECTION 6 – REACTIVE DATA

| STABLE: | CONDITIONS TO AVOID: | |
|---|---|---|
| MATERIALS TO AVOID | | |
| HAZARDOUS DECOMPOSITION PRODUCTS | | |

SECTION 7 – SPILL OR LEAK PROCEDURES

| STEPS TO TAKE IN CASE MATERIALS RELEASED OR SPILLED | |
|---|---|
| WASTE DISPOSAL METHOD | |

SECTION 8 – SPECIAL PROTECTION INFORMATION

| TYPE OF RESPIRATORY EQUIPMENT | |
|---|---|
| VENTILATION | |
| LOCAL EXHAUST: MECHANICAL GEN: | SPECIAL (SPECIFY): OTHER (SPECIFY): |
| PROTECTIVE GLOVES: | EYE PROTECTION: |
| OTHER PROTECTIVE EQUIPMENT | |

SECTION 9 – SPECIAL PRECAUTIONS

| HANDLING & STORAGE PRECAUTIONS | |
|---|---|
| OTHER PRECAUTIONS | |

| PREPARED BY: | TIME: | DATE: |
|---|---|---|
| SITE AUTHORIZATION: | | DATE: |

**Extension 9**    Book       *Classic Accidents*
                   Author     David Farmer
                   Edition    1989
                   Publisher  Croner Publications Ltd

This small book, besides describing numerous examples of accidents, gives helpful advice on preventing them.

**Extension 10**   Book       *The Costs of Accidents at Work*
                   Edition    1997
                   Publisher  Health and Safety Executive

Intended to be helpful to business, this book of case studies should help you realize just how costly accidents can be.

**Extension 11**   Book       *Safety Representatives and Safety Committees*
                   Edition    1996
                   Publisher  Health and Safety Commission

Contains Code of Practice, Regulation, and Guidance notes.

**Extension 12**   Book       *Essentials of Health and Safety at Work*
                   Edition    1994
                   Publisher  Health and Safety Executive

**Extension 13**   Book       *Manual Handling (Manual Handling Operations Regulations 1992 – Guidance on Regulations)*
                   Edition    1998
                   Publisher  Health and Safety Executive

Contains just about everything you might want to know about manual handling, including how to comply with the law.

Many of these extensions can be taken up via your ILM Centre. They will either have them or will arrange that you have access to them. However, it may be more convenient to check out the materials with your personnel or training people at work – they may well give you access. There are other good reasons for approaching your own people; for example, they will become aware of your interest and you can involve them in your development.

# 4 Answers to self-assessment questions

1   The correct statements are:

b   Contract law is relatively unimportant in health and safety matters.

c   Following an accident, an organization may be prosecuted under either criminal law or civil law.

d   European law takes precedence over UK law.

f   The Health and Safety at Work, etc. Act 1974, places an obligation on employers to take care of the health and safety of customers on its premises.

g   Employees have duties to co-operate with employers in meeting the requirements of the law.

i   'As far as reasonably practicable' means that the degree of risk can be balanced against the cost of taking measures to avoid the risk.

2   Safety representatives may be involved in:

■   TALKING to employees about particular health and safety problems;

■   encouraging CO-OPERATION between their employer and employees;

■   carrying out INSPECTIONS of the workplace to see whether there are any real or potential HAZARDS that haven't been adequately addressed;

■   bringing to the attention of the employer any UNSAFE or unhealthy conditions or working PRACTICES, or unsatisfactory WELFARE arrangements;

■   REPORTING to employers about these problems and other matters connected to health and safety in that WORKPLACE;

■   taking part in ACCIDENT investigations.

3   a   Approved codes of practice (ACOPs) – [vii] Issued by the Health and Safety Commission (HSC) as interpretations of regulations, and are intended to help people apply the law in practice.

b   Civil law – [iv] A plaintiff sues a defendant, usually for damages, that is, financial compensation. As an example, an individual may sue an employer if he or she is injured at work.

c   Prohibition notice – [ii] stops, with immediate effect, people from carrying out activities that are considered to involve a risk of serious personal injury.

d Criminal law – [iii] Anyone committing a crime has offended against the state, and is in breach of this. If an organization fails to comply with its statutory health and safety duties, its officers may be prosecuted.

e EU Directives – [vi] Bind member countries to comply with an agreed ruling. They are normally made into national laws by each state.

f Improvement notice – [v] compels an employer to put right conditions that contravene the health and safety law.

g Statute law – [i] Acts of Parliament (such as the Health and Safety at Work, etc. Act 1974), together with a great many 'statutory instruments' or 'subordinate legislation'.

| **Self-assessment 2 on page 59** | 1 | **Under MHSWR, employers must:** | **This includes the process of:** |
|---|---|---|---|
| | | a provide risk assessment | iii identifying the hazard; measuring and evaluating the risk from this hazard; putting measures into place that will either eliminate the hazard, or control it |
| | | b provide health surveillance | i identifying adverse affects; rectifying inadequacies in control; informing those at risk of any damage to their health; reinforcing health education |
| | | c appoint competent persons | iv identifying those with sufficient training, and experience or knowledge and other qualities; requiring them to devise and apply the measures needed to comply with health and safety laws |
| | | d consult employees' safety representatives | ii identifying measures that may substantially affect health and safety; identifying health and safety aspects of new technology; discussing these with the relevant people. |

2 More than one regulation will apply in most work situations. Some you may have identified are as follows.

i Loading bags of flour: [c] Manual Handling Operations Regulations 1992 (MHOR).

ii Supervising telesales: [d] Health and Safety (Display Screen Equipment) Regulations 1992.

iii Running an electrical department in a superstore: [b] Workplace (Health, Safety and Welfare) Regulations 1992 (WHSWR).

   iv Training fork-lift truck drivers in a fuel depot: [a] Management of Health and Safety at Work Regulations 1999 (MHSWR).

   v Supervising an area where there are high levels of dust. [a] Management of Health and Safety at Work Regulations 1992 (MHSWR).

   vi Supervising on a building site: [e] Personal Protective Equipment at Work (PPE) Regulations 1992 (PPEWR).

  3 Under the COSHH regulations, employers have to:

- determine the HAZARD of SUBSTANCES used by the organization;

- assess the RISK to people's health from the way the substances are used;

- prevent anyone being EXPOSED to the substances, if possible;

- if exposure cannot be prevented, decide how to CONTROL the exposure so as to reduce the risk, and then establish effective CONTROLS;

- ensure that the controls are properly used and MAINTAINED;

- examine and TEST the control measures, if this is required;

- inform, INSTRUCT and train employees (and non-employees on the premises), so that they are aware of the hazards and how to work SAFELY;

- if necessary, MONITOR the exposure of employees (and non-employees on the premises), and provide HEALTH SURVEILLANCE to employees if necessary.

  4 Businesses must register with the environmental regulator and comply with the Producer Responsibility Obligations if they handle more than 50 tonnes of packaging and have a turnover of more than £2 million.

**Self-assessment 3 on page 8**

 1 The correct matches are as follows:

| | |
|---|---|
| Accident | Any undesired circumstances which give rise to ill health or injury; damage to property, plant, products or the environment; production losses or increased liabilities. |
| Hazard | The potential to cause harm, including ill health and injury; damage to property, plant, products or the environment; production losses or increased liabilities. |
| Risk | The likelihood that a specified undesired event will occur due to the realization of a hazard by, or during, work activities; or by the products and services created by work activities. |
| Danger | An unacceptable level of risk. |
| Safety | The result of the activities we carry out to keep something or somebody from harm. |

2    a   The seven 'classic' accident types [iii] keep on happening to different people, in different places.

     b   Accidents at work are largely caused by [ii] safety systems out of control.

     c   An organization's health and safety policy statement [i] is the starting point for all accident prevention and health promotion.

**Self-assessment 4 on page 103**

1   The correct statements are:

     b   Proactive safety strategies, rather than reactive ones, are best.

     d   Safe processes, safe premises, and safe materials, are all necessary and important in making workplaces safe.

2    a   A safe SYSTEM of work is the INTEGRATION of people, machinery and materials in a correct working ENVIRONMENT to provide the safest possible working CONDITIONS.

     b   Under HSWA, EMPLOYERS must have regard for the safety of NON-EMPLOYEES who may be affected by the activities of their companies.

     c   All EMPLOYEES have duties: to take REASONABLE care for their own safety and that of others; to CO-OPERATE with their employers in matters of safety; not to INTERFERE with or misuse anything provided for safety.

     d   Every EMPLOYER must make an ASSESSMENT of the health and safety RISKS of work activities to EMPLOYEES and anyone else who may be affected, and record the findings.

     e   MHSWR requires employers to appoint COMPETENT people.

3   Risk ratings are assigned to hazards in order to compare the risks associated with various work operations, and to help decide on the urgency of remedial action required.

4    1   Eliminate the risk.

     2   Enclose the risk.

     3   Install a safety device.

     4   Implement a system of work that reduces the risk.

     5   Provide specific written safety instructions.

     6   Supervise those at risk from the hazard.

     7   Provide training.

     8   Provide general information about safety.

     9   Provide personal protective equipment.

**Self-assessment 5 on page 136**

1    a   Accident prevention shouldn't depend on people always obeying the rules.

     b   Ensure that young persons are trained and supervised.

     c   Inspection and maintenance of equipment are essential.

     d   It's useful to think about what might go wrong.

e  Keep untrained and unauthorized people away from dangerous machines.

f  Keeping the guards in place is not just good practice – it's the law.

g  Equipment that hasn't been in use should be checked.

h  Organization have a duty to protect non-employees.

i  Switches should be well marked and easily accessible.

j  Using untrained operators, or unguarded machines, may be against the law.

2  The two most important points to bear in mind about good housekeeping are that it plays an important role in helping to prevent accidents, and can have a positive effect on the quality and standards of work and behaviour.

3  Some of the ways of reducing the risk from electric shock are the following.

■ Don't leave covers open, or allow untrained or incompetent people to open covers over live electrical parts.

■ Disconnect faulty apparatus and place a 'do not use' label on it.

■ Show all users of electrical machines how to isolate the power from it in case of emergency.

■ Place a well-marked switch or isolator close to every machine.

■ Have all electrical installations checked regularly by a trained electrician.

4  Falls that most commonly occur in workplaces include:

■ people tripping or falling at the same height or level;

■ people falling from one height to another;

■ something falling onto someone.

5  To help prevent ladder accidents, you could:

■ make sure ladders are secured by tying at the top, or else at the sides or bottom;

■ do not allow anyone to work on a ladder without a handhold;

■ check the state of ladders regularly, to ensure they are in good condition;

■ train people to set up ladders at the correct angle: ladders should have a slope of four units up to one out from the base;

■ train people to avoid setting ladders against fragile surfaces, or on insecure footings;

■ make sure the ladders used are right for the job.

**Self-assessment 6 on page 154**

I  The immediate actions are:

a  Assess the situation.

b  Make the area safe.

c  Get help.

d  Give first aid.

2 Investigators need to find out:

- the sequence of events that led up to the accident;
- the system of work that was in operation;
- about any relevant environmental factors;
- what plant and equipment was involved;
- who was present.

They should also:

- take photographs, make sketches, and take measurements of the scene and the relevant features;
- obtain statements, as soon as possible, from all persons who were involved in, or who observed, the accident;
- review the facts, in the light of what has been learned, taking steps to resolve any inconsistencies or conflicting evidence;
- get expert help, if necessary;
- come to a conclusion, if possible, regarding the causes of the accident;
- generate a written report of the accident, which describes what happened, sets out the causes, and recommends changes to prevent a recurrence.
- make the information available to other sites that operate in similar circumstance or use similar equipment.

# ▣ 5 Answers to the quick quiz

Answer 1 Enabling Acts allow (or 'enable') Ministers to issue detailed Regulations at a later date, without the need to have them debated in full in Parliament. Examples are the Health and Safety at Work, etc. Act 1974 (HSWA) and the Environment Protection Act (EPA).

Answer 2 The two main routes are through the civil and criminal courts. The third route is via an employment tribunal.

Answer 3 Directives, which bind member countries to comply with an agreed ruling, are normally made into national laws by each state.

Answer 4 Other examples are: check systems of work frequently to ensure that risks from hazards are minimized; monitor the work environment regularly, to ensure that people are protected from any toxic contaminants; inspect safety equipment regularly; minimize risks to health from 'natural and artificial substances'.

Answer 5    Employees have responsibilities under HSWA to take care for their own health and safety, and that of their colleagues; to co-operate in meeting the requirements of the law including the acceptance of health and safety training; not to interfere with or misuse anything provided to protect their health, safety and welfare.

Answer 6    If the words 'the employer shall' are used, it means that the requirement that follows is compulsory.

Answer 7    To carry out a risk assessment, you must identify the hazard; measure and evaluate the risk from this hazard; and put measures into place that will either eliminate the hazard, or control it.

Answer 8    The purpose of health surveillance is to identify adverse affects early; rectify inadequacies in control, and so reduce the risks to those affected or exposed; inform those at risk, as soon as possible, of any damage to their health, so that they can take action; and to reinforce health education.

Answer 9    A person can be regarded as competent if he or she has 'sufficient training, and experience or knowledge and other qualities, properly to undertake' the role.

Answer 10   The Workplace (Health, Safety and Welfare) Regulations 1992 (WHSWR), and the Health and Safety (Display Screen Equipment) Regulations 1992.

Answer 11   You should consider whether the load must be moved at all, and if so, whether it could be moved by non-manual methods.

Answer 12   Under PPEWR, employers have to ensure this equipment is suitable and appropriate; maintain, clean and replace it; provide storage for it when not in use; ensure that it is properly used; give employees training, information and instruction in its use.

Answer 13   A hazardous substance is virtually any substance in the workplace.

Answer 14   By looking into 'near miss' incidents, a lot may be learned that may help prevent an actual accident in similar circumstances.

Answer 15   Organizations need to have systems – policies, plans and procedures – that are designed to ensure that accidents do not happen. If these systems are inadequate or out of control, then accidents will and do occur.

Answer 16   When safety objectives are set, it is important to know whether, and to what extent, they are being met. To evaluate objectives, therefore, they should be compared with a quantifiable standard.

Answer 17    It means that many of the costs of accidents to an organization are not recognized, and not insured against.

Answer 18    Organizations should control the situation by taking the initiative, rather than
simply reacting to what happens.

Answer 19    Acts of Parliament (statute law); common law or case law; EU Directives.

Answer 20    All employees have duties:

■ to take reasonable care for the safety of themselves and others;
■ to co-operate with their employer in matters of safety;
■ not to interfere with or, misuse anything provided for their safety.

Answer 21    A formal definition of risk assessment is: 'an identification of the hazards present in an undertaking and an estimate of the extent of the risks involved, taking into account whatever precautions are already being taken'.

Answer 22    You might have mentioned:

■ checking that the ladder is secured;
■ not working on the ladder without a handhold;
■ checking to see that the ladder is not weak or damaged;
■ placing the ladder at a stable angle;
■ not placing the ladder against a fragile surface;
■ placing the ladder on a secure footing;
■ using the correct ladder for the job.

Answer 23    While static electricity isn't always dangerous in itself:

■ the shock from static electricity can cause an involuntary movement which
could result in an accident;
■ sparks generated by static electricity can be very dangerous near flammable
liquids, or organic powders.

Answer 24    Suitable questions include:

■ Is it really necessary to move the load?
■ Does it have to be moved manually?
■ What is the risk of injury?
■ How can I eliminate or reduce this risk?

Answer 25    You could have mentioned: flying particles; dust; chemical splashing; flying
molten metal; vapours and gases; radiation.

Answer 26    The simplest reason is that untidy workplaces may contain hazards of many
kinds, including tripping, slipping, and falling hazards.

Answer 27 A good piece of advice is: 'Assume that what might go wrong will go wrong'. In other words, think of all the things that **could** occur.

Answer 28 Assess the situation; make the area safe; get help; give first aid.

# 6 Certificate

Completion of this certificate by an authorized person shows that you have worked through all the parts of this workbook and satisfactorily completed the assessments. The certificate provides a record of what you have done that may be used for exemptions or as evidence of prior learning against other nationally certificated qualifications.

# superseries

## Managing Health and Safety at Work

........................................................................

has satisfactorily completed this workbook

Name of signatory ..........................................................................................

Position ..............................................................................................

Signature ............................................................................................

Date ....................................................................

Official stamp

**Pergamon
Flexible
Learning**

Fifth Edition

# **super**series

## FIFTH EDITION

Workbooks in the series:

| | |
|---|---|
| Achieving Objectives Through Time Management | 978-0-08-046415-2 |
| Building the Team | 978-0-08-046412-1 |
| Coaching and Training your Work Team | 978-0-08-046418-3 |
| Communicating One-to-One at Work | 978-0-08-046438-1 |
| Developing Yourself and Others | 978-0-08-046414-5 |
| Effective Meetings for Managers | 978-0-08-046439-8 |
| Giving Briefings and Making Presentations in the Workplace | 978-0-08-046436-7 |
| Influencing Others at Work | 978-0-08-046435-0 |
| Introduction to Leadership | 978-0-08-046411-4 |
| Managing Conflict in the Workplace | 978-0-08-046416-9 |
| Managing Creativity and Innovation in the Workplace | 978-0-08-046441-1 |
| Managing Customer Service | 978-0-08-046419-0 |
| Managing Health and Safety at Work | 978-0-08-046426-8 |
| Managing Performance | 978-0-08-046429-9 |
| Managing Projects | 978-0-08-046425-1 |
| Managing Stress in the Workplace | 978-0-08-046417-6 |
| Managing the Effective Use of Equipment | 978-0-08-046432-9 |
| Managing the Efficient Use of Materials | 978-0-08-046431-2 |
| Managing the Employment Relationship | 978-0-08-046443-5 |
| Marketing for Managers | 978-0-08-046974-4 |
| Motivating to Perform in the Workplace | 978-0-08-046413-8 |
| Obtaining Information for Effective Management | 978-0-08-046434-3 |
| Organizing and Delegating | 978-0-08-046422-0 |
| Planning Change in the Workplace | 978-0-08-046444-2 |
| Planning to Work Efficiently | 978-0-08-046421-3 |
| Providing Quality to Customers | 978-0-08-046420-6 |
| Recruiting, Selecting and Inducting New Staff in the Workplace | 978-0-08-046442-8 |
| Solving Problems and Making Decisions | 978-0-08-046423-7 |
| Understanding Change in the Workplace | 978-0-08-046424-4 |
| Understanding Culture and Ethics in Organizations | 978-0-08-046428-2 |
| Understanding Organizations in their Context | 978-0-08-046427-5 |
| Understanding the Communication Process in the Workplace | 978-0-08-046433-6 |
| Understanding Workplace Information Systems | 978-0-08-046440-4 |
| Working with Costs and Budgets | 978-0-08-046430-5 |
| Writing for Business | 978-0-08-046437-4 |

For prices and availability please telephone our order helpline
or email

+44 (0) 1865 474010
directorders@elsevier.com